Rowing

NEW
HOLLAND

Rowing

Keith Maybery

First published in 2002 by
New Holland Publishers Ltd
London • Cape Town • Sydney • Auckland
www.newhollandpublishers.com

86 Edgware Road
London W2 2EA
United Kingdom

80 McKenzie Street
Cape Town 8001
South Africa

14 Aquatic Drive
Frenchs Forest, NSW 2086
Australia

218 Lake Road
Northcote, Auckland
New Zealand

ISBN 1 85974 893 7 (hardback)
ISBN 1 85974 936 4 (paperback)

Publisher: Mariëlle Renssen
Managing Editors: Claudia Dos Santos, Simon Pooley
Managing Art Editor: Richard MacArthur
Editors: Simon Lewis, Melany McCallum
Designer: Richard MacArthur
Illustrator: David Vickers
Production: Myrna Collins
Picture Researcher: Colleen Abrahams
Consultants: John McArthur and James Worrell

Reproduction by Unifoto Pty Ltd
Printed and bound in Singapore by Craft Print International Ltd

2 4 6 8 10 9 7 5 3 1

Disclaimer
The author and publishers have made
every effort to ensure that the information contained in this book was accurate
at the time of going to press, and accept
no responsibility for any injury or incon-
venience sustained by any person using
this book or following the advice herein.

Author's acknowledgements

Special thanks must go to my wife Sandra, whose constant love and support, has enabled me to continue to row and coach and to accept the challenge and privilege of writing this book on Rowing. Thank you to all of my family and close friends for their encouragement and support. Special thanks to all my rowing partners, particularly those whose help and inspiration went beyond boats.

Our sincere thanks to Zak Wood, Roger Tobler, Clive Gillman, Graham Cooke, Bernard Frerichs, Darryn Frerichs, Nadine de Kok and Janet Larsen for assisting with the photographic shoot; Mike Cowell for all his help with the photographic shoot; and the Victoria Lake Club in Germiston, Johannesburg, for providing access to their facilities. Thank you Lois O'Brien, Simon Pooley, Richard MacArthur and New Holland Publishers for giving me this opportunity.

Contents

Lore of Rowing

rowing had its beginnings with the Egyptians, Greeks, Romans and Vikings, all of whom had immeasurable influence on the evolution of rowing into a worldwide sport that attracts male and female participants from as young as 10 years old right up to people into their seventies and even eighties. Rowing evolved as a result of a fundamental need for transport, exploration and fishing. The first classical watercraft enabled ancient kings to display their might and prowess to their subjects as well as to their detractors and enemies.

Many centuries before the birth of Christ, and in the times of ancient Egypt, the pharaohs and kings were transported in multi-decked, multiple oared craft, usually powered by over 100 galley slaves. The first rowing festivals were brought about by the inevitable desire and ego of watermen whose competitive spirit inspired a desire to race one another!

Christopher Dodd's *The Story of World Rowing* and Hilton Cleaver's *A History of Rowing* make interesting reading and are highly recommended for their extensive research and insight into the sport. Today the underlying reason for people joining the worldwide rowing family is to enjoy the social contact with like-minded people in a healthy outdoor environment. The added benefit is the sheer joy and satisfaction that comes from skimming over the water in sleek, perfectly engineered rowing boats.

Rowing is the second-oldest organized sport (after athletics), with the first recorded competitive regatta dating back to 1315 in Venice. The sport really took root in England during the late 15th to early 16th centuries as a result of people needing to cross the River Thames, which at that stage had very few bridges. This need gave birth to an inevitable explosion in the number of men turning their hand to oarsmanship, either for their own transport needs or to ferry others across or down the Thames for a fee. The growth of this transport system inevitably led to a breakdown in discipline, which resulted in countless boating accidents. These incidents gave rise to the necessity for watermen to become apprenticed as well as obtain an oarsman's licence — and so it was that the first professional oarsmen took to the water.

Pierre de Coubertin (1863–1937), a French baron and founder of the modern Olympic Games, has special claims on rowing. His countless texts show that rowing held a special place and passion for him, and he cited the sport as 'the ideal discipline'. Not surprisingly,

above 'THE COMING OF THE NORSEMEN' IN 1000AD. THIS TAPESTRY ILLUSTRATES A VIKING LONGBOAT UNDER SAIL AND OAR POWER.

opposite THE 1944 OXFORD-CAMBRIDGE BOAT RACE, SUPPORTED BY ROWERS AND SCHOLARS ON THE BANKS OF THE THAMES.

rowing was included in the Olympics since the first modern Games in 1896, and is the second-oldest and third-largest sports code at the Olympics, following in the wake of track-and-field athletics and the various swimming disciplines.

Men and women of all ages participate in rowing; it introduces them to a pleasant physical pursuit which they can enjoy in beautiful and tranquil surroundings. For others, it can be a highly competitive sport requiring many strenuous hours of preparation in order to achieve their high levels of technical proficiency. Important life skills are also learned from the interaction with their rowing crews, along with the practise of self-discipline, self-determination and commitment to a team effort. The strong mental conditioning that is attained is also of benefit in every walk of life, along with increased stamina achieved through peak physical fitness.

When you start rowing on your own or with a crew, and become more accomplished, you will experience a personal physical and spiritual sense of fulfilment which is all part of 'messing around' in rowing boats.

In order to get a sense of the pleasure that is in store for you as an aspirant rower, find the opportunity to sit and watch a well-drilled rowing crew in action, or a single sculler gliding over the water. Enjoy the mixture of physical precision combined with a sense of poetry in motion. Like all skill-based endeavours, it is true of rowing that performance is directly related to hours of practice and mental concentration.

ROWING HAS BEEN INCLUDED IN THE OLYMPIC GAMES SINCE THE FIRST MODERN EVENT OF 1896. IN THE 1908 LONDON OLYMPIC GAMES, THE ROWING EVENTS WERE HELD AT HENLEY-ON-THAMES (above), AS WAS THE CASE IN THE 1948 GAMES. DUE TO CHANGES IN INTERNATIONAL RACING REGULATIONS, HENLEY WOULD NOT BE ABLE TO HOLD AN OLYMPIC REGATTA IN FUTURE, AS STILL WATER IS NOW REQUIRED FOR FAIR COMPETITION.

Racing & Regattas

The standard straight-line racing distance of 2000m (2180yd) applies to the Olympic Class and most world events, such as international and national championships. Regattas often take place on waterways that, by virtue of their specific geographical structure and limitations, dictate the possible race distance. The Oxford-Cambridge rowing race (known universally as The Boat Race) is contested over a distance of approximately 7km (4.3 miles) between Putney and Mortlake on the River Thames in London. The Henley Royal Regatta, on the other hand, has a race distance restricted to 1 mile and 550yd (approximately 2km), which is the straight-line distance available on the Henley Reach, Henley-on-Thames.

A PAIR OF MEN'S EIGHTS LEAVES THE START AT THE HENLEY ROYAL REGATTA WITH THE FAMOUS TEMPLE ISLAND IN THE BACKGROUND.

AN ARMADA OF MOTOR LAUNCHES FOLLOWS THE ANNUAL OXFORD AND CAMBRIDGE BOAT RACE CREWS ON THE THAMES IN LONDON.

Races

As with any sport, in rowing there is always the ritual of preparing for a race, inspecting the boat prior to putting it on the water, and tightening up whatever parts need to or can be tightened. The last words of encouragement from the coach ensure that everyone in the crew has a clear idea about the race plan. The pre-race warm-up should include stretching and flexibility exercises, after which the crew (or sculler) take to the water and continue to prepare for the race as they row towards the starting point. Invariably, en route to the start, the crew (or sculler) will include a few practice race starts.

Where possible the boats are held by the stern from a starting pontoon. Alternatively, a floating start procedure can be adopted, with the bow of each boat being brought into alignment as well as being perpendicular to the course prior to the starter's orders.

Once in the 'start', the coxswain (and/or bow rower) of a crew boat, or the single sculler, may raise their hand to indicate that they or the crew are not ready; they can do this up till the time the starter conducts the roll-call of competitors (crews or scullers). After the last crew has been named in the roll call, the starter raises his red flag and gives the warning command ('Attention') and, after a pause, calls 'Go!' as he drops his red flag.

At some courses 'traffic lights' have supplemented the flag. In the case of a false start, a bell is rung and the starter waves a red flag to recall the crews or scullers.

Crews are only allowed one false start each, after which they will be disqualified from the race if they break the start early for a second time. Many races allow restarts in the event of an equipment breakage, as long as it occurs within 100m (109 yd) of the start.

A championship race course is set out much like a swimming gala, with each racing crew or sculler being allocated a racing lane. Each lane is 12.5—15m (14—16 yd) wide and is typically demarcated by rows of buoys, which are set at 10m (11 yd) intervals. This racing course system or layout is known as the Albano System. Straying from a lane and interfering with another boat, regardless of intent, is punishable with disqualification by the umpire.

The winner of a race is the boat whose bow crosses the 'finish line' first, as monitored by judges, often with a photo-finish camera. The umpire must raise a white flag at the end of the race to signify that it has been completed in accordance with the rules and that there has been no protest by any crew or official.

A considerable amount of 'Coastal' racing occurs in the South of England using wider boats with sliding seats on rivers, estuaries, harbours and open sea. Surfboat rowing, another open sea pursuit, is a popular form of racing in Australia, and many athletes make the transition from one form of rowing to another.

THE 1996 OLYMPIC ROWING COURSE AT GAINESVILLE NEAR ATLANTA, GEORGIA, IS A TYPICAL 2000M RACING COURSE CLEARLY SHOWING THE LANE MARKER BUOYS. THE STERN IS BEING HELD AT THE START.

THE MEN'S HEAVYWEIGHT EIGHTS CREWS AT THE FINISH OF THE 1997 WORLD CHAMPIONSHIPS IN FRANCE, WHERE THE USA CLEARLY WON BY 'A CANVAS' (THE DISTANCE FROM THE TIP OF THE BOWS TO THE FIRST MAN IN THE BOAT). THE FINISH LINE IS HIGHLIGHTED ON THE WATER SURFACE BY A STREAM OF AIR BUBBLES EMERGING FROM A SUBMERGED PIPE, MAKING THE JUDGES' JOB MUCH EASIER.

A PAIR OF SCULLERS ENJOY A RECREATIONAL ROW WITH THEIR COMPANIONS. RECREATIONAL ROWING ALLOWS FRIENDS, FAMILIES OR COUPLES THE CHANCE TO GET OUT ON THE WATER TOGETHER TO ENJOY NATURE WHILE TAKING IN SOME PHYSICAL ACTIVITY. PICTURED ABOVE IS A WIDE-BEAMED BOAT, WHICH IS MORE STABLE ON THE WATER AND ALLOWS THE COUPLES TO CARRY PICNIC HAMPERS AND SPARE CLOTHING FOR THEIR TRIP.

Recreational rowing

Recreational rowing is practised throughout the world and is becoming increasingly popular. Not all rowing has to be done with the idea of head-to-head racing in mind. Naturally, there are those who love the experience and exhilaration of top competition but, equally, there are many participants who have neither the time nor the drive to become too serious about competitive rowing. The latter simply want to row for the benefit of the physical activity and the enjoyment of beautiful and tranquil surroundings.

Recreational rowing is for family and friends who gain pleasure out of spending time together in a boat. There are many waterways in the world that will provide endless opportunities for enjoying sociable rowing trips. One can use the standard racing shell for the purpose of recreational rowing on flat waters but, for rowing tours and longer excursions, custom-made boats (or 'Gigs') are used.

Gigs are wide-beamed boats which can be up to 1 x 11m (1.09 x 12 yd) and can carry a crew of four rowers and a coxswain. Gigs are incredibly stable craft, a fact which does away with the difficulty of maintaining boat balance, something that is of constant concern in the racing shell. For leisure trips the participants don't want to be bothered with boat balance, and quite possibly many people on a social party would struggle to keep a racing shell balanced. Because of the wide-bodied design of gigs, the crew is also able to stow clothing, food and other provisions on board to cater for some home comforts during a day trip or a longer overnight excursion.

The crew can be as leisurely as they like, rowing for as many or as few kilometres a day as the mood takes them; they have the freedom to stop off for 'tea' or the 'odd pint', as the inclination arises. This makes for a wonderful blend of exercise and sociability. Where excursions of longer duration are undertaken, the rowing crew is normally supported by a backup crew who travel ahead of the intrepid rowers in a motor vehicle, preparing campsites and meals as well as organizing the social affairs of the holiday.

Recreational and touring rowing is plain fun and, whether you are a social rower or a serious competitor, here is the way to truly enjoy rowing leisurely surrounded by nature's beauty.

The need to row

Rowing can become a drug for those athletes who discover this hidden gem of the sporting world. You may retire from rowing as the demands on your time increase due to work and family commitments, but, inevitably, the sport will lure you back, either as a regular, more competitive endeavour or as an occasional and social diversion.

The sport is, however, unusual and often inaccessible due to geographical and financial reasons. This makes rowers something of an elite group — yet definitely not elitist. Rowers are quick to welcome new members into their fold, particularly since their legion is underpinned by a colourful heritage that embraces both watermen and gentlemen, both scholars and scoundrels.

The Oxford-Cambridge boat race continues to be one of the world's best known and most historic sporting events. It received vast worldwide exposure as a result of Dan Topolski's best-selling account of the 1987 campaign, *True Blue* (made into a motion picture in 1996). The book and movie, although slated in many quarters for a loose grasp of the truth, provides a wonderful insight into the world of rowing and, especially, two of the oldest rowing cultures in the world. For inspiration and motivation, *True Blue* is essential reading or watching.

True Blue follows the fortunes of a beleaguered Oxford crew following the withdrawal of their prize American rowers. Oxford coach Topolski secured a win against the favourites, Cambridge, partly owing to the luck of winning the toss, in addition to brilliant tactical choices and decisions made by the coaches and cox, who made best use of the recent heavy rains that had fallen. This highlights the possibility that rowing's inexperienced underdogs can still triumph, that technical superiority doesn't always translate to victory on the day. It's an element that always provides

THE LADIES EIGHTS PASS THE STEWARDS ENCLOSURE AS THEY APPROACH THE FINISH LINE AT THE PRESTIGIOUS ANNUAL HENLEY ROYAL REGATTA.

THE TWO CREWS COMPETING IN THE OXFORD-CAMBRIDGE BOAT RACE, EGGED ON BY THEIR COXES, APPROACH THE HARRODS DEPOSITORY.

an edge in the sport. There is always a battle to be fought. It might well be over within the first minute or two, when a strong crew gains a good lead. But at least at the drop of the starter's flag, or the crack of the pistol, the crews know that there is some chance of an upset. The same can't be said for all sports.

But, who would choose such a demanding sport? Well, clearly, almost anyone, for its appeal is so wide. The loner, the individual who prefers isolated endeavour, can lose him- or herself in single-sculling. The extrovert or achiever can single-scull to put himself on the line, test his ability on his own, much like a long-distance runner. For the team player, or the more social individual, the demands of perfect synchronisation of stroke and effort make rowing one of the most challenging and demanding of sports. There can be no weak links if a crew hopes to succeed. The demands on one's time are great, as are the logistics of organizing training sessions for a crew; however, the rewards are incomparable when it all comes together and your craft thrusts mightily through the water, defying nature.

And nature is another reason why we row. Out on the water you're away from man's constructed society (as long as motorboats are out of sight). You're alone with your thoughts or with the sounds of the heaving mass or your crew puffing through stroke after stroke. It's you and nature. No unfair advantages. You're under your own steam. Paddling your own canoe, so to speak. Answering nature's call to extend yourself to your limits of physical exertion while maintaining timing and technique. That's why we row. But why do we strive to succeed? Simple. Everyone wants to taste success ... and throw that damn cox into the drink!

A TRIUMPHANT CAMBRIDGE CREW THROW THEIR COX INTO THE THAMES.

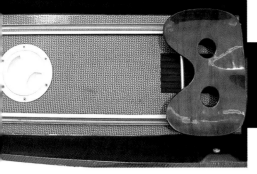

Know your Boats

It is safe to say that, as long as there is a reasonable body of water present, you will find rowing clubs in most cities around the world. The sport will also almost certainly be formally organized and properly run, which means that most clubs have good social amenities, changing-rooms and associated facilities. The more established clubs have gymnasiums in addition to indoor rowing machines, and you can expect to be welcomed into a congenial environment that will provide you with encouragement, support and adequate facilities to aid your progression in the sport.

Your initial encounter with the world of rowing clubs will have you intrigued as you enter an extra-large shed and see rack upon rack of long, missile-shaped boats. As you move around the boat shed the coach will familiarize you with the boats, also referred to as 'racing shells', which rest upside down on their racks waiting to be carried (upside down) outside to the jetty. These 'shells' are long, sleek, smooth-finished and have hard exteriors.

Beginners are often confused about the terms rowing and sculling. 'Rowing' is the generic name of the sport, and participants are called 'rowers'. The difference in the methods of propelling boats forms the basis of sculling or rowing. In sculling the individual propels the boat with a pair of sculling oars — one oar is held independently in each hand. 'Single-sculling' is when you are in a boat on your own, naturally using two oars. 'Scullers' form part of larger crew boats of either two or four people, each operating two oars.

In 'rowing' (or sweep oar), the individual controls and propels the craft by handling a single rowing oar with both hands. It is always practised by even-numbered crews of either two, four or eight team members, called 'rowers'.

The difference between the various boat types is evident in the diagrams and classifications of boat categories on page 18. The 'outriggers' (often just referred to as 'riggers') each hold an oar and, as a result, offer an indication as to the boat type.

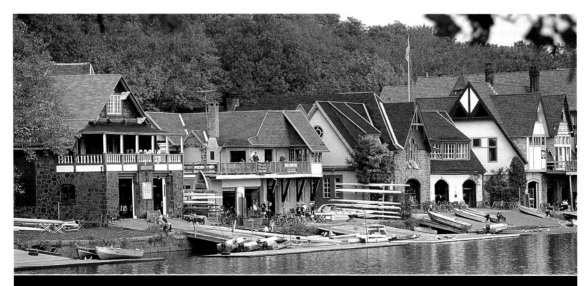

above THE BOATHOUSE ROW, SCHUYLKI RIVER, PHILADELPHIA, USA, IS A FINE EXAMPLE OF BOATHOUSES ENHANCING THE RIVERBANK.

opposite THE UTILITARIAN NATURE OF AN EIGHT-OAR ROWING BOAT; COMPACT AND BUSINESSLIKE, WITH NO SPACE FOR FRILLS OR FLOURISHES.

Boats categories

Boat classes	Names	Configurations	Dimensions	Minimum race mass
Eight oar with coxswain	Eight (8+)		Length: 16.8–17.6m Beam: 0.56m	96kg
Octuple scull with coxswain	Octuple (8x+)		Length: 17–17.6m Beam: 0.56m	100kg
Quadruple scull without coxswain	Quad (4x)		Length: 11.78–12.89m Beam: 0.43m	52kg
Quadruple scull with coxswain	Coxed Quad (4x+)		Length: 12.89–13.65m Beam: 0.43–0.46m	54kg
Four oar without coxswain	Coxless Four (4-)		Length: 11.78–12.89m Beam: 0.43–0.46m	50kg
Four oar with coxswain	Coxed Four (4+)		Length: 12.89–13.65m Beam: 0.46–0.47m	51kg
Double scull	Double (2x)		Length: 9.40–9.98m Beam: 0.33–0.35m	27kg
Pair oar without coxswain	Pair (2-)		Length: 9.40–9.98m Beam: 0.33–0.35m	27kg
Pair oar with coxswain	Coxed Pair (2+)		Length: 10.0m Beam: 0.37m	32kg
Single scull	Single or Skiff (1x)		Length: 7.78–8.33m, Beam: 0.27–0.29m	14kg

(abbreviations for boat names are given in brackets)

AN EIGHT IS VERY LIGHT FOR A BOAT THAT IS NEARLY 18M (60FT) LONG, BUT ONCE YOU ADD THE CREW, IT CAN TOTAL OVER 1000KG (2200 LB).

Beam and length

'Beam' refers to the boat's width and 'length' refers to exactly that. Boat lengths and widths vary essentially so that they can carry different average body masses of the crew. The wider and longer the boat, the greater its ability to handle displacement. The larger the person or the crew-members, the larger the boat needs to be in each class of craft.

Coxless and coxed

'Coxless' refers to the boat having no provision for a coxswain; a coxless four, therefore, has no cox. The 'coxless' type of craft includes boats for four oars, and pair-oars — and normally all classes of sculling boats exclude coxswains. This includes the quad, the double and the single. The coxed quad scull is, however, typical of novice or school events.

'Coxed' refers to a boat that is normally steered by a coxswain. In coxed boats the coxswain has his own 'seat' from which to control the boat. This can be either in a seated position at the stern of the boat or in a lying position facing into the bow of the boat. The coxswain steers with his or her hands by pulling or pushing on two cords that run along either side of the boat down to the rudder.

top A FOOTBOARD WITH STEERING MECHANISM FOR COXLESS BOATS.

above AN OCTUPLE HAS SIXTEEN OARS AND RIGGERS.

A STERN-COXED BOAT. THIS COX USES A MODERN SPEAKER SYSTEM.

What is an octuple?

A number of countries have adopted an 'octuple' into their range of equipment for schoolchildren, who are given their first taste of crew activity when being taught to scull. A 'rowing eight' is converted into a convenient craft for equipping young children in their efforts to scull. This craft is a very useful way to shepherd eight young scullers (aged 12–14) up or down a river or on any other open piece of water.

By introducing this boat, you reduce the exorbitant cost of purchasing an entire fleet of single sculls as well as maximizing your coaching efforts, since eight people are able to scull in the same boat together. An octuple also ensures that 'eights' are given the opportunity to handle extra rigging. At the same time, the octuple can be used for both sculling and rowing.

The bow and the stern

In a yacht, canoe or powerboat you are seated facing the BOW end of the craft, the so-called 'sharp end'. The STERN is the end behind you, where the motor or rudder is located. However, in a rowing or sculling boat you are seated facing the STERN, with your back to the BOW end of the boat.

The sharp nature of the bow has resulted in legislation that demands that a 'bow ball' (a solid, white rubber ball that looks much like the end of a 'trailer hook') be used at all times during practice and racing. The bow ball goes some way to minimize the risk of serious injury should you row into another person, and it helps to reduce the damage done if you collide with another craft. However, depending on the speed you are travelling, the amount of damage can still be severe. The bow ball also makes it easier for judges to tell which craft crossed the finish line first.

Bowside and strokeside

It is important to know your right from your left in a rowing boat. The following applies when viewed from the stern of the boat — when you are facing the bow, which has the bow ball attached to it:

■ The right-hand side of the boat is the 'bowside', known in maritime terms as the 'starboard' side, which has green as its colour code.

■ The left-hand side is the 'strokeside' or port side, with red as its colour code.

To help you remember the above, think of the phrase, 'Is there any red port left in the bottle?'

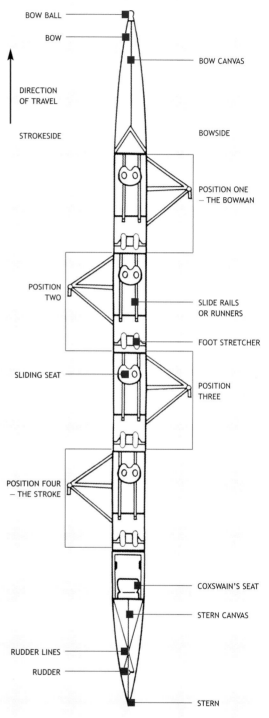

BOW BALL
BOW
BOW CANVAS
DIRECTION OF TRAVEL
STROKESIDE
BOWSIDE
POSITION ONE — THE BOWMAN
POSITION TWO
SLIDE RAILS OR RUNNERS
FOOT STRETCHER
SLIDING SEAT
POSITION THREE
POSITION FOUR — THE STROKE
COXSWAIN'S SEAT
STERN CANVAS
RUDDER LINES
RUDDER
STERN

above A COXED ROWING FOUR VIEWED FROM ABOVE.

left A BOW WITH A BOW BALL; IN THE BACKGROUND IS A STERN.

The racing craft

There are very few restrictions imposed upon boat builders. The International Rowing Federation's Rule 27 of part IV on Boats and Construction states that: '... construction and dimensions of boats and oars shall, in principle, be unrestricted but remain subject to the limits laid down by Rule 1, Paragraphs 1 and 2' (which cover the definition of rowing). The only real restrictions imposed are those contained in By-law 1.4, which states that no substances or structures, like riblets, which are capable of modifying the natural properties of water or the surface layer of the water, shall be applied to the hull. By-law 2.7 imposes certain restrictions on individual boat masses.

Racing shell materials

The traditional lightweight hand-crafted wooden structures of sleek rowing boats have slowly evolved into state-of-the-art man-made materials, with the aid of technology drawn from the aerospace industry. Racing boats are light in weight yet are exceptionally strong and robust. However, they are nonetheless easily damaged. The laminated sandwich construction of modern-day boats combines the use of the key materials of Kevlar, unidirectional carbon fibre, and Nomex honeycomb. These materials are also extremely durable and long-lasting, at the same time ensuring that longitudinal strength is maximized and flexibility is kept to an absolute minimum.

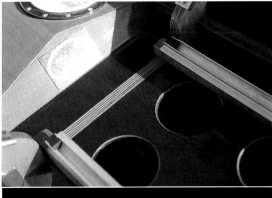

A RACING SHELL WITH LAMINATED PLYWOOD DECKING AND RIBS.

High-grade epoxy resins help to form what becomes at least a triple-laminated sandwich construction. In the final stages of completing the lay-up of the wet materials, the vacuum formed in a mould is heat cured at considerable temperatures, which results in an exceptionally strong yet light and stiff shell. The pre-impregnated carbon inner deck materials are added to the shell, ensuring that the craft has a higher degree of overall rigidity and longitudinal strength.

Maintenance

The overall life expectancy of modern boats has been substantially increased and, at the same time, their upkeep and maintenance has been even more substantially reduced. These days scratches, holes or tearing of the shell can be quickly and easily remedied. Even boats which have been literally cut in half can be restored and, thereafter, continue to be used for years.

In the normal course of events boats need to be kept clean and as soon as scratches and holes occur they should be repaired. Commercial twin-pack epoxy resin products, which are available from most hardware stores, are quite adequate for running repairs or on-the-spot repairs. Some parts of the boat need regular checking and maintenance, while many of the moving parts may need regular replacing.

It is essential for all parts of the boat to be checked regularly — ideally every time you go onto the water — to monitor their general condition as well as to make sure that they are securely in place.

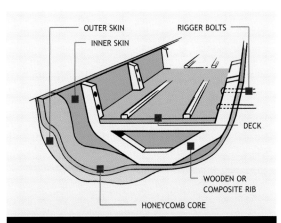

OUTER SKIN   RIGGER BOLTS
INNER SKIN
DECK
WOODEN OR COMPOSITE RIB
HONEYCOMB CORE

A CROSS-SECTION THROUGH A MODERN RACING SHELL.

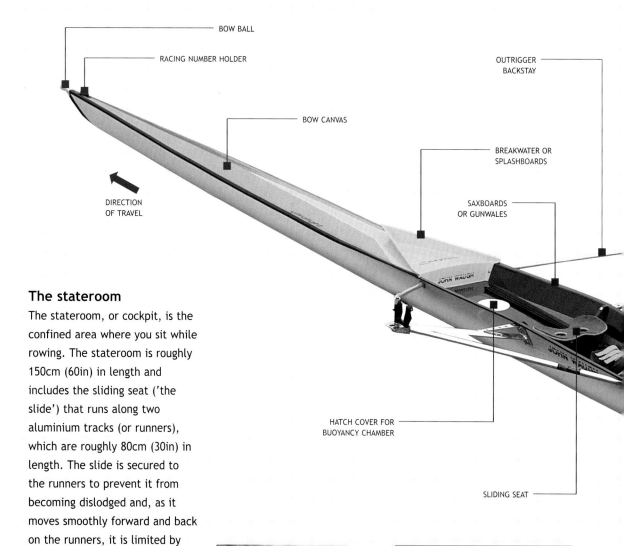

BOW BALL

RACING NUMBER HOLDER

OUTRIGGER
BACKSTAY

BOW CANVAS

BREAKWATER OR
SPLASHBOARDS

DIRECTION
OF TRAVEL

SAXBOARDS
OR GUNWALES

HATCH COVER FOR
BUOYANCY CHAMBER

SLIDING SEAT

The stateroom

The stateroom, or cockpit, is the confined area where you sit while rowing. The stateroom is roughly 150cm (60in) in length and includes the sliding seat ('the slide') that runs along two aluminium tracks (or runners), which are roughly 80cm (30in) in length. The slide is secured to the runners to prevent it from becoming dislodged and, as it moves smoothly forward and back on the runners, it is limited by the frontstops and backstops.

The prime purpose of the slide is to enable you to use the full potential power of your legs. The seat's changing position enables the rower to adjust the body position to take full advantage of the mechanical efficiency available from their height, reach and body mass in the seated position.

THE SLIDING SEAT OR 'SLIDE', ON WHEELS.

THE OUTRIGGERS, SWIVEL AND GATE.

Any keen rower should get to know the names of all the parts of the boat. The names of the various parts remain the same for all classes of boat, like the single scull pictured below.

The stretcher (footboard)

The stretcher, or footboard, secures your feet in the boat and is made up of two parts: a pair of track shoes (or restraints) and an adjustable backing board. The stretcher can be easily adjusted and fixed to suit the flexibility, height and length of your legs. Adjustment of the shoes on the board enables you to set the height of the feet and legs so that you can optimize your leg drive. It is important that the angle of the stretcher is set carefully. The flexibility of the ankles, tendons and other leg joints plays an important role in maintaining a consistent rhythm as well as in generating power.

Serrated nylon strips hold the stretcher in place, with one positioned on the bottom of the boat and another two on opposite sides of the boat. In older boats, holes are aligned and secured with wing nuts.

For the purpose of steering coxless boats, one of the rowers assumes the responsibility of steering the boat with the aid of a nylon-covered cable which is attached to a moveable shoe on one of the boat's foot stretchers. The cable runs from that foot stretcher through to the rudder.

A STRETCHER, OR FOOTBOARD.

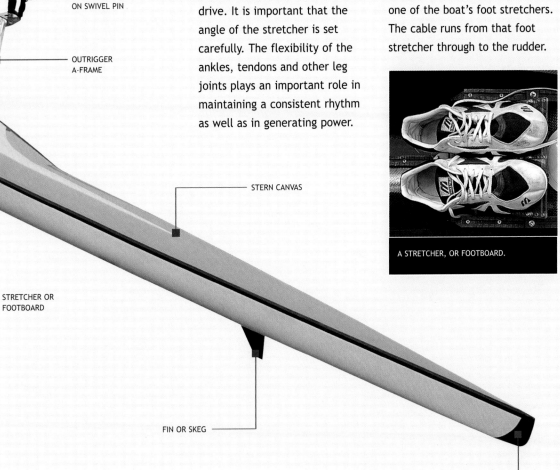

SWIVEL AND GATE ON SWIVEL PIN

OUTRIGGER A-FRAME

STERN CANVAS

STRETCHER OR FOOTBOARD

FIN OR SKEG

STERN

Riggers and rigging

As you become more skillful in the technique of rowing and sculling, so the need for specific rigging adjustment becomes increasingly important. There are many advanced and technical rowing books that deal with the subject in greater depth but, for the beginner's purposes, we will introduce the fundamentals and the process of setting up a boat and then run through the technical jargon. My advice is that you should leave the job of rigging to your coach. He or she has been trained to deal with all the finer points surrounding optimum rigging recipes, as well as for being able to teach you the 'ins and outs' of the rowing stroke (or cycle).

The process of rigging aims to ensure that you are given the best opportunity to take advantage of your latent physical potential, and this is achieved by making adjustments to the boat that will enable you to be comfortable in the boat. The rigging process will also assist you to acquire a high level of technical ability, which will enable you to achieve optimal levels of boat speed.

If you are not supervised by a coach, or if you want to know more about rigging to enable you to customize your own setting, Steven Redgrave's *Complete Book of Rowing* has a superb chapter on rigging.

A ROWING EIGHT HAS FOUR RIGGERS ON EACH SIDE OF THE BOAT.

Outriggers

The outriggers (usually referred to simply as 'riggers') of rowing and sculling boats are adjustable and thus allow you a number of options, similar to a bicycle's gear system, although rowers have to make adjustments to the outriggers and the oars beforehand, without the luxury of changing gears while rowing. These adjustments make it possible to increase or reduce the available leverage. The oars are secured in swivels (oarlocks) attached to the craft's outriggers by a 'swivel pin' (also known as a 'thole pin').

You need to know what effect the changes will have on you as well as the dynamics of what you are dealing with. Like bicycles, boats need their gear ratios to be set specifically for the person doing the work. Leverage adjustments are similar to selecting the correct gears on a bicycle, so it's hardly surprising that in rowing we refer to the process as 'gearing'.

Individual gearing settings are made to the outrigger to help produce optimum crew performance and boat speed. These settings are made to allow the crew or sculler to cope with the actual race distance as well as external influences such as wind.

The coach will keep his eye on ensuring that you are able to move through as wide and effective an arc as possible, in order to bring about the most efficient length of rowing stroke possible.

The following are important rigging terms to know:
Span (sometimes called spread)
The span is set with the use of a tape measure, with the measurements being taken from the centremost point of the boat to the centremost point of each swivel pin of the outrigger.
Stern pitch (the forward setting of the pin)
The stern pitch influences the swivel angles on the outrigger (and hence the blade or spoon pitch or angle) relative to the water. These settings help perfect the entry and extraction of the spoon in the water.
Lateral pitch
The lateral pitch is the in-and-out setting of the 'swivel pin', which influences the constancy of the blade or spoon cover (the amount of water that covers the spoon) during the stroke cycle. The considerations for

lateral pitch adjustments to the swivel pin of the outrigger are similar to those mentioned for adjustments to stern pitch.

Inboard and outboard settings

The higher and lower gearing settings have an effect on 'leverage' and are made to the outrigger. Finer leverage adjustments, which will either increase or reduce leverage, are made to the inboard/outboard ratio on the oar. These settings can also dramatically affect the arc and 'length' of the stroke. Setting the gearing is the combined action of adjusting the span as well as setting the inboard/outboard ratio on the actual oar.

Oar pitch on the oar

The oarmaker usually sets the pitch angle of the oar at zero degrees, but will never set it greater than two degrees. In conjunction with the stern pitch, this pitch setting takes care of the angle of spoon entry to the water.

The swivel (oarlock)

The swivel is responsible for keeping the oar or scull in place. The sleeve is positioned in the swivel before it is secured by the gate. The gate is a metal pin which closes the top of the U-shaped swivel. There are several variations of swivel available, the most common is shown in illustration D, along with four pairs of inserts. These inserts enable between one and seven degrees of stern to bow pitch adjustment to be made to the swivel without affecting anything else.

Swivel height

Swivel height is important in that it affects the handle height of the oars throughout the stroke. The body masses of the crew or individual sculler influence the displacement of water by the boat and the height of the boat in the water. Adjustments to the rigger height and the swivel height accommodates this displacement, and it thus becomes necessary for height adjustments to be made to fine-tune the boat trim according to actual displacement of the water by the boat and crew. The most conventional method of measuring swivel height is to set the 'swivel sill' height at 14–18cm (5.5–7in) above the lowest point on the sliding seat. Fine height adjustments are possible for raising or lowering the swivel with the height spacers.

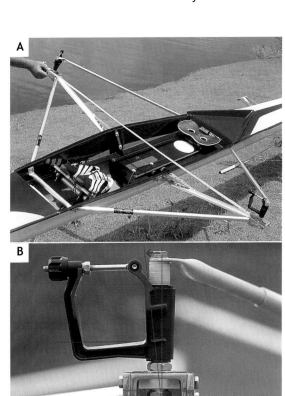

A

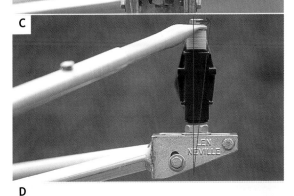

B

C

D

A USING A TAPE MEASURE TO CHECK THE SPAN SETTING.

B STERN PITCH AND SWIVEL HEIGHT AS VIEWED FROM SIDE OF BOAT.

C LATERAL PITCH AS VIEWED FROM BOW OF BOAT.

D SWIVEL AND THE INSERTS NEEDED TO ADJUST STERN PITCH.

A rowing or sculling craft is either propelled by a solitary rower or by crews of two, four or eight rowers, using (in most cases) carbon fibre oars that correspond with the technical competence of the rower. The modern-day rowing and sculling oar has come a long way over the last 50 years. Modern materials like carbon fibre have made it possible to manufacture oars that are stronger, much lighter and allow for leverage adjustments.

Terms for oars and sculls

Modern rowing and sculling oars are highly adjustable to suit the specific needs of the crew and the rowing conditions they face. The following technical terms are used to identify the various parts of these oars.

■ **Inboard** is the length of handle that exists on the oar or scull, as measured with a measuring tape, from the outermost edge of the oar or scull handle to the inside of the oar collar or button. Adjustments to the inboard distance are made to increase or decrease the leverage available on the oar handle. Adjustments will always take into account the existing span of the riggers.

■ **Outboard** is the measured length of oar shaft that exists between oar collar and the tip of the spoon, or blade. Adjustment of the inboard (leverage) impacts upon the outboard distance.

■ **Oar/scull length** is the overall length along the axis of the oar or scull from the centre of the spoon to the tip of the handle.

Oars and sculls are made in various lengths, and recent developments also allow for the adjustment of the overall length (length = inboard + outboard).

■ **The spoon** or **blade** of the oar has evolved through considerable design changes over the years. They started out as long, narrow wooden spoons before changing to the wider Macon-shape of the 1970s. Today the universally known 'Cleaver' spoon is used, so called because the spoon looks like a butcher's cleaver. The principle advantage of the Cleaver over the Macon spoon is that it does not slip on its entry into the water — this encourages an instant and firm connection at the beginning of the stroke cycle. If pitched correctly, the blade also finds its own depth in the water.

Cleaver rowing oar (top) and Cleaver scull.

The portion of the blade marked 'inboard' is kept inside the rigger, while the 'outboard' part is always above the water. The blade is the only part that should enter the water during a normal stroke. The sleeve is plastic to protect the shaft from damage arising from hard and persistent contact with the collar.

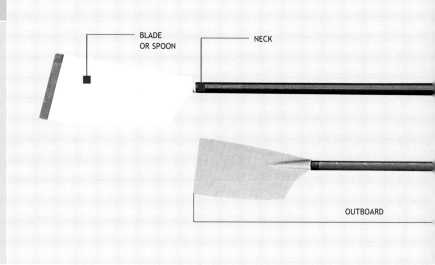

BLADE OR SPOON

NECK

OUTBOARD

Oar construction

Multiple laminations of wood have given way to spun carbon materials in the manufacture of rowing oars and, with the advent of carbon fibre, oars that are 50–60% lighter than their former counterparts have evolved. Like the modern racing shell, they are light in weight yet are exceptionally strong. Like rowing shells, oars do not have any restrictions placed upon them other than (purely for safety reasons) those relating to the edges of the spoons. Rowing oar spoon thickness has been set at 5mm (0.2in), while sculling oar spoon thickness must be at least 3mm (0.1in).

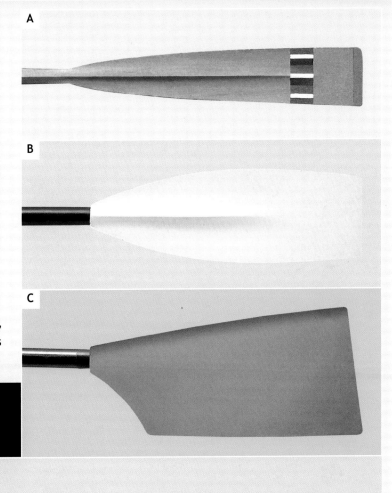

A

B

C

A A PRE-1950 SPOON BLADE.

B A MACON SPOON BLADE.

C A CLEAVER SPOON BLADE.

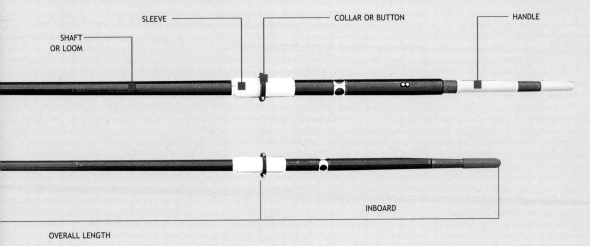

SHAFT OR LOOM

SLEEVE

COLLAR OR BUTTON

HANDLE

INBOARD

OVERALL LENGTH

Safety and Clothing

Know the local water rules

Rowing accidents do occur but, in general, an accident will happen because someone on the water has not followed the rules, has ignored dangerous weather conditions or has failed to become fully conversant with the local waterway conditions. Diligence in personal safety is a number one consideration for rowers throughout the world, along with the safety of all their fellow water users. To achieve this there are a few priority steps to be taken each time you take to the water and especially when you visit a new waterway.

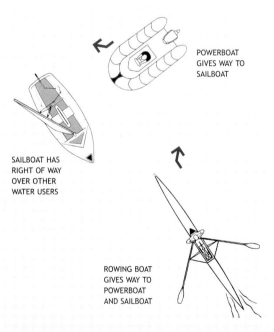

POWERBOAT GIVES WAY TO SAILBOAT

SAILBOAT HAS RIGHT OF WAY OVER OTHER WATER USERS

ROWING BOAT GIVES WAY TO POWERBOAT AND SAILBOAT

Important international water rules

- Before taking to the water you must familiarize yourself with the local water rules.
- Be prepared for any emergency to yourself or a fellow water-user and know the whereabouts of the first-aid equipment as well as the telephone numbers of all emergency services.
- Rowing boats should keep left and give way to motor and sailboats. The reality, however, is that a rowing boat cannot be easily stopped at full speed, making it difficult to 'give way'. The wash from bigger boats also affects a rowing boat's stability.

You must be able to swim

The rowing and sculling boats used in this sport are not required to carry personal flotation devices. Therefore, for your own safety and, because the wearing of personal flotation equipment while rowing is not practical, it is of great importance for any person involved with rowing to be a reasonably competent swimmer in open waters. This is especially true for single sculling. Due to the nature of the waterways you are likely to row on, it is essential that you are able to swim at least 50m (55 yd) fully clothed, or 400m (436 yd) in swimming trunks. You should also be able to correctly re-enter your sculling boat after falling into the water. Coaching boats should always carry life jackets and/or personal flotation devices, plus a 25m (27 yd) rope for assisting rowers in distress.

top THE 'SAFE POSITION' FOR NOVICE SCULLERS, HANDS OVERLAPPING, OARS TOUCHING AND RESTING ON THE KNEES.

above THE RIGHT OF WAY RULES ON THE WATER.

right THE HATCH-COVER ON THE DECK AIDS BUOYANCY.

opposite EVEN ACCOMPLISHED CREWS SUCH AS THE OXFORD AND CAMBRIDGE BLUES CAN SINK IN ROUGH WATER, DESPITE SAFETY MEASURES SUCH AS EMPTYING WATER FROM THEIR CRAFT.

Before you take to the water, observe the following situations

- Is the jetty area clear enough for you to boat on?
- Take note of the movement of other craft – their whereabouts and their comings and goings.
- Prevailing weather conditions – wind, clouds, the possibility of a thunderstorm or lightning, and the likely existence of mist and/or fog?
- Your own equipment – is everything in good working order? Make sure that you have a spanner with you.
- Is the bow ball secure and are the heels of the shoes secured by the safety straps?
- Does the coaching boat have life jackets and rope?
- If you are going on the water after dark, make sure that you are in the company of another sculler, and that your boat is fitted with a flashing red light similar to the type used by cyclists.

above THE FOOTBOARD MUST BE ATTACHED TO THE SHOES WITH HEEL RESTRAINTS BEFORE GETTING ONTO THE WATER.

When you are out on the water, remain observant at all times

- Be certain of following the local water rules.
- Constantly observe what is ahead of you. Look ahead (over your shoulder) every 8–10 strokes.
- Give way to faster, oncoming boats and, if there is any doubt or pending danger, yell 'Ahead!'
- Always attempt to row in the company of other crews and scullers. Avoid going out on your own in isolated or lonely waters.

Respect the weather conditions

Weather conditions play a significant role in the life of a rower and you need to pay attention to changing moods. Gather weather information from your fellow club-members and get to know everything possible about reading cloud patterns. Never be too proud to err on the side of caution and common sense!

Lightning and thunderstorms can be particularly dangerous. Watch out for darkening clouds and a sudden change in temperature. At the earliest signs of adverse conditions or evidence of lightning, do not hesitate: LEAVE THE WATER IMMEDIATELY!

It is equally important for you to avoid rowing in murky, misty and/or foggy conditions. Allow your common sense to take charge and you will avoid losing your way in the dark and, potentially, crashing into someone or something, like the riverbank!

Rough water can also be hazardous – you need to judge your rowing competence carefully before setting out on the water.

top RED OR WHITE CYCLING LAMPS SHOULD ALWAYS BE USED AT NIGHT.

above A SINGLE SCULLER OR A COXLESS CREW SHOULD CHECK AHEAD EVERY 8–10 STROKES TO SEE IF THEIR PATH IS CLEAR.

How do you get back into the boat after falling out?

You need to stay with your boat as it is exceptionally buoyant and you can rely on it as a flotation device. If you have been separated from your boat or it is sinking, then an oar can be used as a flotation device.

Take hold of the boat and/or the rigger and compose yourself prior to attempting to re-enter the boat.

1 Place the oar closest to you across the boat's beam.
2 Reach across and retrieve the oar on the opposite side of the boat.
3 Hoist your body over the saxboard aft of the rigger.
4 Draw the oar handle towards the sliding seat deck.
5 Keep a hand on the oar handle nearest you.
6 Hoist your torso onto the boat's bow deck.
7 Sling one of your legs over the bow deck and hang your feet in the water.
8 Find your balance.
9 Take hold of the oar handles.
10 Reposition yourself on the sliding seat.
11 Place your feet back into your shoes.
12 You are ready to continue with the next strokes.

The most secure and stable position for a sculler to assume is where the oars are at 90 degrees to the boat and the sculler has a firm hold of both oar handles, which are rested on slightly raised, flexed knees. A similar position can be used in a sweep oar boat.

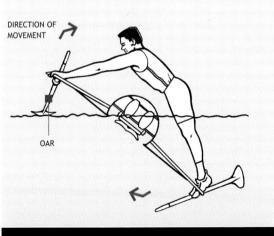

DIRECTION OF MOVEMENT

OAR

YOU CAN RIGHT YOUR BOAT IN THE WATER FAIRLY EASILY BY STANDING ON THE RIGGER AND PULLING THE OPPOSITE RIGGER TOWARDS YOU.

top HOLDING ONTO THE OPPOSITE SIDE OF THE BOAT FOR BALANCE, REACH ACROSS FOR THE OTHER OAR.

centre HAVING RIGHTED THE FAR OAR, SLIDE INTO THE BOAT USING THE NEARSIDE OAR FOR STABILITY AND BALANCE.

bottom STILL HOLDING THE NEARSIDE OAR, TURN AND SIT INTO THE BOAT IN WHAT'S KNOWN AS THE 'SAFE' POSITION.

Personal care

It is advisable to wash your body and your clothing after every training session or race, especially your hands before eating.

As with any form of intense exercise, care should be taken to ensure that you adequately hydrate your body during training and races: drink plenty of liquids.

Blistered hands are a very common complaint suffered by rowers as a result of the continuous hand and finger actions used in the stroke cycle, as well as technique difficulties with the squaring and feathering of the spoons. Care should be taken to keep the damaged skin clean and sterile. It may be necessary to release the fluid from large blisters by piercing the area with a sterile needle.

Surgical spirits can be used to harden the palms of your hands. Covering the hands with plaster is generally unhelpful, although cycling mitts can help to ease any discomfort.

Clothing

Each rowing club has its own formal clothing attire, as well as distinctive formal racing attire. Racing gear will in all likelihood include a tracksuit and certain wet-weather clothing as well as specific clothing for use on cooler days when you need extra protection to prevent sickness or cold muscle injury. A good pair or two of running shoes are a must for inclusion in your kit bag.

Training attire is generally very casual, although in certain instances the local club etiquette may require that the club uniform is worn during training sessions. The weather also dictates what is worn and there are a few pointers to be considered regarding the appropriate apparel.

Hot weather protection

- Hot and humid climatic conditions, where ultraviolet radiation is a problem, will necessitate shielding of the arms, body and head.
- Light, nonrestrictive Lycra clothing dissipates heat and provides a snug body-figure fit. This is preferable to loose and floppy clothing, which could cause the hands and fingers (or the wheels of the sliding seat) to become snarled-up at various stages during the stroke cycle.
- Cycling shorts (without the chamois) are very popular, as are full-body Lycra tri-suits.
- Sunglasses and a suitable cap or hat are advisable.
- Use a sunscreen protection in excess 20 SPF.
- Socks prevent foot disease.
- Regardless of the time of year, never leave home without a spare set of clothing.

A TRI-SUIT IS COMMON ATTIRE FOR RACING AND MOST CLUBS WILL HAVE ONE IN THEIR OWN COLOURS. SOCKS HELP TO PREVENT THE TRANSMISSION OF FOOT DISEASES.

Cold weather protection

In cold weather you need to be equally as careful as you are during hotter weather. Nonetheless, it is difficult to persuade rowers to dress properly in cold weather conditions. This is because rowers don't 'feel the cold' as the body produces a great deal of heat while rowing. Coxswains and coaches are, on the other hand, particularly susceptible to the cold because they are relatively inactive compared to their crews and are thus more likely to dress warmly.

Cold and wet conditions reduce the blood flow to the skin. The body wrestles between trying to maintain body temperature against the cold outside influences of wind and ambient temperature. Occasional dowsing from cold water does not help and may lead to frostbite and hypothermia.

About one-third of your body heat is lost through the top of your head, so wearing a hooded top, balaclava, hat or cap will help you store heat.

Thermal garments or, alternatively, several layers of clothing, will protect you from the cold. The advantage of wearing several layers of clothing is that you trap heat between the layers and can add or remove layers when needed. You should keep your lower back warm and protect it from exposure to cold water, as it is an area prone to a strain or injury that can seriously incapacitate any rower.

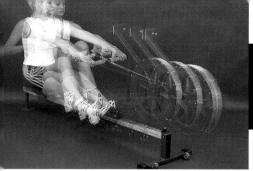

The Basics

most gymnasiums and rowing clubs offer rowing machines on which patrons can learn the basic elements of the rowing stroke on dry land. These rowing machines are known as 'rowing ergometers', or 'ergos'.

There are a variety of models of ergometer that are commonly available. These machines are really useful to help the rower get to grips with the basic rowing techniques. Situated in a gym (as opposed to on the water), the ergometer will give you the benefit of close personal attention from a coach or personal trainer, who can observe your stroke from close quarters as well as demonstrate nuances of technique to you. This will enable you to learn the language of rowing as well as affording you the opportunity of discussing and understanding all the intricacies of the sport before you venture off dry land.

The basics of the rowing stroke

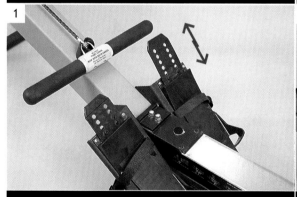

top A MOVING HEAD ERGOMETER AIMS TO REPLICATE THE BOAT'S MOTION.

Step 1 AFTER YOU HAVE SEATED YOURSELF ON THE SLIDING SEAT OF THE ERGOMETER, SET YOUR FOOT HEIGHT SO THAT THREE HOLES ARE SHOWING ON THE SLIDING ADJUSTER. LIGHTLY STRAP YOUR FEET IN. KEEP YOUR LEGS STRAIGHT AND LET YOUR ARMS HANG LOOSE AND COMFORTABLY AT YOUR SIDES (SEE PICTURE 4).

opposite SINGLE SCULLS RACKED AND WAITING TO HIT THE WATER.

Step 2 SWING YOUR ARMS UP UNTIL THEY ARE HORIZONTAL, THEN LOWER THEM TO YOUR SIDES. REPEAT 40 TIMES IN 40 SECONDS.

Step 3 SWING ARMS UPWARD AND RAISE YOUR KNEES. THE SEAT SLIDES FORWARD: SHINS ARE VERTICAL AND ARMS HORIZONTAL.

Step 4 WITHOUT PAUSING, STRAIGHTEN YOUR LEGS. PAUSE FOR ONE SECOND WITH YOUR KNEES FLAT, THEN BEGIN AGAIN. REPEAT THIS 100 TIMES, EACH CYCLE TAKING TWO SECONDS.

Arm draw exercise

Step 1 TAKE HOLD OF THE OAR HANDLE IN THE FIRST TWO JOINTS OF YOUR FINGERS. HOLD THE HANDLE LIGHTLY, NOT TIGHTLY, AS THE CABLE PULLS YOUR ARMS AWAY FROM YOU.

Step 3 MAINTAIN THE 'DINING-ROOM CHAIR' BODY POSTURE. ALLOW THE TENSION OF THE ERGOMETER'S DRAW CABLE TO EXTEND YOUR ARMS UNTIL THEY ARE APPROXIMATELY HORIZONTAL IN FRONT OF YOU.

Step 2 WITH YOUR KNUCKLES, HANDS AND ARMS ON A LEVEL PLANE, DRAW THE HANDLE TO YOUR SOLAR PLEXUS. KNEES FLAT, SIT AS IF IN A DINING-ROOM CHAIR. RELAX YOUR SHOULDERS AND OPEN YOUR CHEST.

Step 4 WITHOUT A PAUSE, DRAW THE HANDLE BACK TO YOUR SOLAR PLEXUS, BUT USING ONLY YOUR FINGERS. REPEAT THIS ACTION UNTIL THE TECHNIQUE BECOMES SECOND NATURE.

Many people think of rowing as a sport in which pulling on the oars provides the driving force. However, competitive rowing with sliding seats involves pushing with your legs in order to lever the boat through the water, as opposed to pulling the water past the boat. Lifting and lowering your knees introduces the concept that the strength or pushing power of your legs does the real work in rowing. The arms and body then provide the link to the oar as well as the means of inserting and extracting the spoon.

The complete rowing stroke

The rowing stroke comprises two specific phases: a) the drive phase, and b) the recovery phase.

These exercises should develop a feel for the concept of lifting and lowering your knees, as well as the essential role these actions play in the rowing stroke. These leg actions facilitate the movement of the sliding seat between the front- and backstops.

These two actions form a significant part of the complete rowing stroke. Straightening the legs provides most of the power in the drive phase, while lifting the knees is a major part of the recovery phase.

Leg drive and recovery positions

The preceding arm draw exercise represents the completion of the drive phase and the start of the recovery phase. An increasing amount of sliding seat movement can then be 'added' to this stroke cycle.

There are five basic sliding seat positions, or reference points, which define the amount of seat motion and, therefore, leg drive (distances will vary depending on the individual rower's height).

Fixed slide

No movement of the slide. The legs should remain straight and flat.

Quarter slide

Roughly 20cm (8in) of forward movement by the sliding seat.

Half slide

Roughly 40cm (16in) of movement by the sliding seat along the runners.

Three-quarter slide

Roughly 60cm (24in) of forward movement by the slide and your body.

Full slide

Full forward motion on the slide to the frontstops.

THE QUARTER SLIDE POSITION SHOWS THAT THE SEAT HAS LITERALLY MOVED A QUARTER OF THE WAY TOWARDS THE FRONTSTOPS.

AT THE HALF SLIDE POSITION THE ANKLE AND KNEE ANGLES ARE BOTH AT ROUGHLY 90 DEGREES.

FOR THE THREE-QUARTER SLIDE POSITION, THE LEGS COMPRESS UNTIL THE SLIDE IS THREE-QUARTERS OF THE WAY TO THE FRONTSTOPS.

AT THE FULL SLIDE, FRONTSTOPS OR CATCH POSITION, THE SHINS ARE VERTICAL. TAKE CARE NOT TO BOUNCE OFF YOUR FRONTSTOPS.

Step 1 THE 'CATCH' REFERS TO THE SPLIT SECOND WHEN YOUR HANDS ARE RAISED TO INSERT THE SPOON AS YOU ACCELERATE THE OAR TO DRIVE THE BOAT FORWARDS. THE FULL POWER OF THE LEGS IS THEN TRANSFERRED TO THE OAR HANDLE. KEEP A FIRM BODY WITH YOUR ARMS OUTSTRETCHED AND YOUR HANDS AT KNEE HEIGHT. THE OAR HANDLE IS HELD LIGHTLY (NOT TIGHTLY) IN THE FINGERS. A QUICK CATCH IS ESSENTIAL, OR ELSE YOU WILL SLOW THE BOAT DOWN.

Step 2 THE KNEES AND LEGS ARE THRUST DOWNWARD IN THE LEG DRIVE WHILE THE ARMS REMAIN OUTSTRETCHED. THE BODY HAS NO SWING AT THIS POINT AND MUST REMAIN 'FIXED' IN POSITION. YOU SHOULD 'HANG ON THE OAR HANDLE' AS YOU CONTINUE TO DRIVE WITH YOUR LEGS, KEEPING YOUR BODY POSTURE ALMOST UPRIGHT. AT THIS POINT THE BACK AND ARMS PROVIDE THE CONNECTION BETWEEN THE DRIVE OF THE LEGS AND THE OAR HANDLE.

Step 3 AS THE LEGS STRAIGHTEN, YOUR UPPER-BODY POSTURE REMAINS FIRM BUT YOU BEGIN TO LEAN BACK SLIGHTLY, ALLOWING ONLY 15–20 DEGREES OF TOTAL BODY MOVEMENT. ONCE YOUR LEGS ARE COMPLETE-LY STRAIGHT THE PULLING POWER OF THE ARMS TAKES OVER. AT THIS POINT YOU DRAW THE HANDS TOWARDS THE SOLAR PLEXUS, WHILE OPENING YOUR CHEST AND SHOULDERS.

Step 4 AT THE END OF THE DRIVE PHASE THE HANDS DROP TOWARDS THE LAP TO EXTRACT THE BLADE (OR BLADES) SQUARELY FROM THE WATER. AT THIS POINT THE FOREARMS SHOULD BE HORIZONTAL AND YOUR WRISTS FLAT. THE UPPER BODY SHOULD BE IN THE DINING-ROOM CHAIR POSITION, WITH YOUR CHEST OPEN, SHOULDERS BACK AND YOUR ELBOWS POINTING SLIGHTLY OUTWARDS.

The recovery phase

The recovery or rest phase is the preparation period for the next drive phase. During this phase your hands rise until your arms are horizontal and your knees lift until you shins are vertical. This period allows the athlete time to catch their breath and relax their muscles while the boat's momentum carries it onwards through the water. The movement in the recovery phase can be described as essentially 'hands-body-slide', although some coaches prefer to emphasise raising the knees.

5

6

Step 5 THE KNEES ARE INITIALLY KEPT FLAT AS THE HANDS LEAD THE ARMS AWAY AS QUICKLY AS POSSIBLE UNTIL THEY ARE FULLY STRETCHED OUT. THEY CONTINUE TO MOVE SMOOTHLY TO THE POINT WHERE THE HANDS APPROACH THE MID-SECTION OF THE SHINS. THE BACK REMAINS STRAIGHT, BUT IT ROCKS FORWARD TO THE CATCH POSITION.

Step 6 AT THIS POINT DURING THE RECOVERY THE BODY POSTURE REMAINS FIRM AND UPRIGHT AS THE KNEES START TO LIFT FLUIDLY AND CONTINUOUSLY. THIS ALLOWS THE SLIDING SEAT TO TRAVEL SMOOTHLY FORWARD TO THE FRONTSTOPS, AND THE HANDS BEGIN TO RISE UP TOWARDS THE CATCH UNTIL THEY ARE HORIZONTAL.

Sculling

In the initial stages of learning to row the best approach is to first master the skills of watermanship associated with sculling. This is best achieved in a double scull, partnered by your coach in the bow position, leaving you in the stroke seat. This allows the coach to balance the boat for you, leaving you to focus your attention on learning the basics. After two or three outings in the double you should be capable of trying your hand at single sculling.

Naturally, you can begin your learning experience in a single scull if you choose or have sufficient confidence in yourself. Once you have reached a good level of proficiency in sculling then the conversion to sweep oar rowing is fairly straightforward.

From boathouse to jetty

It might seem overly simplistic, but moving a single scull from the shed to the jetty (and then back again) is an important procedure for the rower to learn. Handling your equipment with care is essential to keep it in good condition, and following a structured set-up procedure will help to get you in the right physical and mental state for your time on the water. Knowing how to setup your single scull on the jetty will allow you to

progress to handling larger boats with the help of your crew-members. You should start by taking your sculling oars from the rack and placing them on the jetty near the point from where you intend to embark on the water. Regardless of where your boat is stowed, the first task is to open the gate of the swivel that is closest to you. Ideally, you should open both gates.

BEFORE YOU EVEN THINK OF PICKING UP YOUR BOAT, NO MATTER WHERE IT IS STOWED, YOU MUST FIRST OPEN THE SWIVEL GATE CLOSEST TO YOU, ALTHOUGH IT IS RECOMMENDED THAT YOU OPEN BOTH GATES.

How to handle your boat

Depending on the actual rack height on which your boat is stowed, you have one of two options for removing the boat from its rack.

First option

The simplest method of all is to ask someone (like your coach) to help you take your boat to the jetty.

One person holds the boat at the midpoint of the bow deck and the other takes up a similar position on the stern deck. Then you simply lift and carry the boat through to the jetty, making certain that the riggers are kept clear of doors, people and other boats.

Second option

You can also single-handedly carry your boat supported on your shoulder. It is assumed that the boat is positioned on the boat rack between shoulder and hip height. The centre and the balance point of a single scull is towards the stern of the runner deck. It is assumed that the bow and the boathouse door are to your right when facing your boat.

Step 1

Face the boat. Take up a position slightly in front of the pin (towards the bow). Stretch your right arm over the top of the boat and take hold of the rigger backstay that is the furthest from you.

Step 2

Your left hand is placed approximately 30cm (12in) sternward of the pin on the side of the boat closest to you.

Step 3

Lift the boat from its rack and take a step or two backward away from the rack.

Step 4

Use the momentum of the boat to roll it onto your left shoulder, supporting it at the same time with both hands. Be careful to avoid knocking into people and doors. Any wind will add to your difficulties.

above THE EASIEST AND SAFEST WAY TO CARRY YOUR BOAT IS TO ASK SOMEONE TO HELP YOU.

step 1 HOLD THE BOAT FIRMLY AND LIFT IT OFF THE RACK.
step 2 ROLL THE BOAT ONTO YOUR SHOULDER.
step 3 YOU CAN NOW CARRY THE BOAT FROM THE BOATHOUSE.

BEGINNERS SHOULD ALWAYS CARRY THEIR BOAT WITH ASSISTANCE.
REMEMBER TO KEEP AN EYE OUT FOR THE FIN OR SKEG'S POSITION.

Launching your boat
Handling your boat with assistance

It is fairly simple to launch your boat if you have had assistance in carrying it to the jetty. Bear in mind that, when rowing on a tidal river, the direction to leave and approach the pontoon is subject to the direction of the tide at the time, as well as the wind factor. Your bow should point 'upstream' in both cases.

Step 1

Position yourself and the boat so that the bow is facing the direction in which you intend to row.

Step 2

Gently lower the boat into the water. Take care to make sure the boat touches the water evenly and ensure that the fin clears the side of the pontoon.

Step 3

One person holds the rigger of the boat that is closest to the jetty, while the other person collects the oars and returns to the boat.

Handling your boat without assistance
Step 1

Position yourself and the boat so that the bow is facing the direction in which you intend to row. To lower the boat you need to grip the riggers at a point as close to the saxboard as possible.

Step 2

Roll the boat away from you towards the water. Stop the lowering action at your knees. Be on the lookout for wash from other vessels on the water.

Step 3

Bending your knees, you should continue to lower the boat gently until it is resting on the water.

1

2

3

step 1 POSITION YOURSELF AT THE HALFWAY POINT OF YOUR BOAT, GRIPPING THE RIGGERS AS CLOSE TO THE SAXBOARD AS POSSIBLE.

step 2 HOLD YOUR BOAT ON THE SAXBOARDS AT THE RIGGER MOUNTING — DO NOT HOLD IT BY THE FOOT STRETCHER OR DECKING.

step 3 GENTLY LOWER THE BOAT INTO THE WATER, USING ONE HAND TO GUIDE THE HULL CLEAR OF THE LANDING JETTY.

Your first time in a scull

It is vital that once you have taken charge of your sculling oars that you should never let go of them. They provide the crucial balance in the boat, much like the pole for a tightrope walker.

After a successful boat launch

top WITH THE SWIVEL GATES OPEN AND FACING THE STERN OF THE BOAT, PLACE THE JETTY-SIDE OAR INTO THE SWIVEL WITH THE BUTTON ON THE COCKPIT SIDE OF THE GATE. CLOSE AND TIGHTEN THE GATE.
middle SLIP THE OPPOSITE OAR INTO THE SWIVEL, WITH THE BUTTON ON THE COCKPIT SIDE OF THE GATE.
bottom YOU MAY LEAVE THIS OAR RESTING ACROSS THE BOAT'S BEAM WITH THE HANDLE ON THE JETTY.

Step 1 Bow of the boat is to your right-hand side. Your coach will hold the jetty-side rigger as you place the sliding seat three-quarters of the way towards the bow. Pickup the strokeside oar handle, pushing the handle until the collar meets the swivel.

Step 2

Take hold of the bowside oar, then couple the oar handles together firmly in your right hand, spoons facing up in the feather position (flat on the water) and almost in the finish position. Place both feet at the edge of the jetty.

Step 3

Place your right foot onto the runner deck and into the centremost point of the boat. Place your left foot into the boat next to your right foot. Stand balancing for a moment while holding your oar handles.

Step 4

Sit down on the seat, holding your sculling oars together with one hand. Then stretch your legs forward and place your feet on top of your shoes on the stretcher. Do not let go of the oars!

TO BALANCE THE BOAT WHILE STEPPING INTO IT, HOLD BOTH HANDLES TOGETHER IN ONE HAND. USE THE OTHER HAND TO BALANCE YOURSELF.

THE CORRECT ADJUSTMENT OF THE FOOTBOARD IS ESSENTIAL TO ASSIST THE ROWER TO PRODUCE EFFECTIVE STROKE CYCLES.

Getting adjusted in the boat

In your first year or two of rowing, the standard rigging settings for the club's rowing equipment are prescribed by your coach. As you advance you can incorporate specific rigging to suit your needs. Individual 'rigging' will help you to use the correct technique, thus ensuring the most efficient use of your physical potential. The sequence that your coach is likely to follow in setting you up correctly begins with making sure that you are comfortably and correctly seated.

- Know where the **frontstops** are: in the catch position it is where the seat is towards the boat's stern.
- Know where the **backstops** are: in the finish position it is where the seat is towards the boat's bow.
- Make sure that you have the correct leg room.
- Your foot stretcher will be set to allow you to place the sculling handles into the sides of your body.
- At the frontstops your shins should be vertical.
- Your weight should be on the balls of your feet.
- Your legs should be compressed to allow the sliding seat to come within comfortable reach of your heels, with the sliding seat below your shoulders.

The correct oar handle height

The handle should be level with the solar plexus and the top of the forearms should be parallel with the water or the gunwale. The oar handles should be held in your fingers, not gripped by your hands.

Holding your sculling oars correctly

Place your thumbs over the ends of the handles to enable you to provide outward pressure of the button against the swivel. Forefinger and thumb meet at the end of the oar handle. This hand placement is essential for maintaining boat balance. Hold the sculling oars lightly with your fingers, while your forearms and hands are held on the same horizontal plane as your flat wrists. To ensure a proper grip, place the underside of the knuckles along the top of the oar, with your fingers wrapped underneath. The fingers should extend halfway around the handle. Oars come with varying handle sizes for athletes with smaller hands.

'Feathering' the sculling oar means that the spoon or blade angle is parallel with the water and is face-up. The spoon is held flat, on the feather, during the recovery phase of the stroke. At the other end of the scale you will be required to 'square' the spoon or blade prior to executing a rowing stroke. The spoon will turn through 90 degrees so that it can be dipped vertically into the water. Beginners should initially row with square spoons. Only after a few hours of coaching, should you attempt to add the feathering technique to your rowing repertoire.

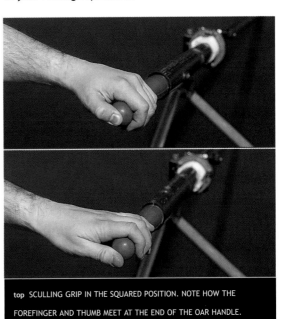

top SCULLING GRIP IN THE SQUARED POSITION. NOTE HOW THE FOREFINGER AND THUMB MEET AT THE END OF THE OAR HANDLE.
above SCULLING GRIP IN THE FEATHERED POSITION.

On the Water

Taking your first strokes

When preparing for your first strokes on the water you will understandably be anxious. Commanding a narrow craft on the water is not as easy as it looks from the sidelines. The thought of taking a dip in cold water is neither physically nor psychologically pleasant.

Before you take your first strokes there are a few do's and dont's which you must take into account. It will be quite normal for you to be drawn into worrying about a variety of matters beforehand, so for the first half-hour or so your coach should present you with a number of challenges. These first encounters may be somewhat daunting.

In the boat for the first time it is natural to ponder what you will need to do with your hands and your legs, how you will balance the boat and whether you can face the prospect of taking a tumble out of the boat and being forced to swim to safety!

During your first few moments in the boat you will find yourself responding to the boat's movement and your instant reactions will cause you to make a few misjudgements. The most misleading of all the sensations is when the boat lurches to one side. Your instinctive response will be to focus your attention — and, at the same time, your body weight — in the direction of the 'problem'. You need to remain calm and relaxed so that you can recover your balance and your composure, which you do by taking care of the problem with the opposite hand to the direction in which you have an imbalance.

above THE 1997 WORLD CHAMPION SINGLE SCULLER, JAMIE KOVEN, DEMONSTRATES DURING WINTER TRAINING THE DEDICATION AND CONCENTRATION REQUIRED TO ACHIEVE HIGHER HONOURS. HOURS OF PRACTICE ENABLE KOVEN TO ACHIEVE PERFECT BLADE HEIGHT AT THE CATCH.

opposite EARLY MORNING AND EVENING TRAINING SESSIONS ARE COMMON PRACTICE AMONGST ROWERS. THESE ARE THE MOMENTS WHEN THE SPORT TRULY GETS INTO YOUR BLOOD.

Which hand does what?

Sculling requires the hands to cross over one another when the oars are at 90 degrees to the boat. Each country's national rowing federation usually decides on the relevant convention and makes the decision on which hand should lead and which hand should follow. The leading hand must assume a position above the trailing hand in order for the spoons to be synchronized. Single scullers, on the other hand, may make their decision based on personal preference.

Forward and aft hand movements, and the importance of developing a consistent hand action during the 'crossover of the hands' in both directions, is a matter of technique that needs early clarity.

In double and quad sculling, the need for conformity of hand movement (in order to maintain a balanced

boat and to ensure that the application of the stroke by the crew-members is as synchronized as possible) demands that the crew adopt the same hand action in accordance with their country's convention of which hand leads forward in sculling. Until recently the Western world seemed to adopt the 'left hand leading' approach, while the Eastern bloc opted for the right hand to lead (referred to as 'left over right' and 'right over left' respectively).

Whichever approach is adopted, however, will have no bearing on the final result of the stroke.

Ready yourself!

Relax as you sit in the boat and prepare to take your first strokes. Be aware that your natural reaction to the actions of the boat and oars are likely to pose some difficulties that you need to be prepared for.

The boat lurches over to one side
Your reaction

You let go of the oar handles, making a grab for the saxboards. The oar handles will go free, the boat will overbalance and you will fall into the water.

What you need to do

Never let go of the oar handles! Always keep the oar handles in your fingertips.

top LEFT HAND LEADING, OR LEFT OVER RIGHT. above A QUAD SCULL DEMONSTRATING THE LEFT-OVER-RIGHT CONFORMITY OF THE CREW'S HANDS.

A spoon gets submerged during the stroke

The boat tilts to your left- or right-hand side. One of the scull handles is forced into your lap. The other scull handle moves vertically and upwards.

Your reaction

Expect to be confused for a moment ... and you may be inclined to continue to apply force to the hand that is in your lap. However, that will only add to your problems by causing the boat to lurch severely to one side and, in all likelihood, probably overturn.

What you need to do

Focus your attention on your upper hand. Place some downward pressure on the oar handle and, as you do this, the opposite hand will be raised to meet the upper hand. The boat will return to an even keel.

The boat will be at its most stable when the oar handles are one above the other at the backstops position. It is therefore advisable to avoid allowing the hands to part from one another. If you carry on fighting with the oar handle then you should expect to go for another swim! When the handles are held together you can do nearly anything you like in the boat. The oars will balance the boat fairly reliably. This is advised for when you want to, or need to, take a breather when out on the water.

Pictured on this page are a few unconventional activities you can accomplish in your boat. Each of these will help your confidence and watermanship.

Essentials of boat balance

Boat balance is fundamental to rowing and sculling and, much like riding a bicycle, once it has been learned it is never forgotten. There is a great deal of satisfaction in sitting in a boat which is well balanced and where your own sense of balance is so well tuned that your rowing ability is actually enhanced. The process of developing a sense of balance is honed over many sessions in the boat. However, in the early phases of your progress you are likely to have some anxious as well as exciting moments.

From the very first strokes that you take right throughout the rest of your rowing career you will continually dwell on what to look for and expect from the concept of 'good balance'. The double scull will be used in the following demonstrations of how best to achieve balance.

When attempting to balance the boat make sure that you do one thing — relax. RELAX. RELAX. That's the key word. Again, imagine being seated on a dining-room chair. Keep your head and body still as you move with the boat.

Establish personal points of balance by:

- Holding the oar handles lightly under your fingertips.
- Sitting squarely on your buttocks (bottom).
- Resting your body weight on the balls of your feet.
- Parting the knees not more than 8–10cm (3–4in).

WITH YOUR HANDS HOLDING THE OARS TOGETHER IT IS POSSIBLE TO DO ALMOST ANYTHING IN THE BOAT AS THE OARS — HELD IN PLACE TOGETHER — SERVE TO MAINTAIN THE BOAT'S BALANCE.

TO DEMONSTRATE HOW STABLE THE BOAT IS WITH THE OARS JOINED, TIE THE HANDLES TOGETHER AND THEN STAND UP AND TURN AROUND. NATURALLY YOU SHOULD TURN FAIRLY SLOWLY. THIS DRILL WILL BOOST YOUR CONFIDENCE IN YOUR BALANCING ABILITY AND IN YOUR BOAT.

Boat balance drills

In order to be competent at executing multiple sculling and rowing strokes you must be able to execute single strokes as well as possess the knowledge of processing one stroke at a time. At the same time you need to be able to find and control your boat balance. There are five checkpoints for practising balance and executing single and multiple stroke exercises.

Checkpoint one — fixed slide position

The body posture is relaxed and upright, shoulders and chest open, seated as if you were on a dining-room chair, hands level with your solar plexus, legs straight. The spoons are flat on the water. This is known as the 'backstops' ('back chocks'), or 'fixed slide', position.

Boat balance at checkpoint one

When practising this exercise in a stationery boat you should attempt to use square blades. Continue by applying downward pressure with your hands on the oar handles so that the spoons clear the water. Apply equal weight with your fingers and lateral pressure with your thumbs to help balance the boat. Ensure that your body weight is distributed evenly on your buttocks and the balls of your feet.

Checkpoint two — quarter slide

The body posture is firm and upright yet relaxed, arms fully stretched, knees raised to the point where the sliding seat has moved 20cm (8in) forward, at which point you pause. The hands and oar handles are stretched out in front of you and below your knees. The oar spoons are feathered (flat) and resting on the water. Your body weight is on the balls of your feet. You are now paused at the 'quarter slide position'.

Boat balance at checkpoint two

At the quarter slide position, apply downward pressure with your hands on the oar handles so that the spoons are clear of the water and feathered. Your body weight is on the balls of your feet and you apply outward pressure with your thumbs and fingers, balancing the boat. Your weight must be distributed evenly on your buttocks, on your fingertips, and on the balls of your feet. Keep the upper body still.

Boat balance will come from ensuring that you apply lateral pressure to the buttons and swivel pins with your thumbs and fingers as well as from maintaining an even distribution of your body weight. At all costs avoid collecting water on the spoons as this will affect your stroke as well as your boat balance.

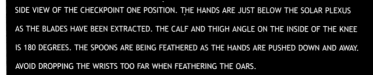

SIDE VIEW OF THE CHECKPOINT ONE POSITION. THE HANDS ARE JUST BELOW THE SOLAR PLEXUS AS THE BLADES HAVE BEEN EXTRACTED. THE CALF AND THIGH ANGLE ON THE INSIDE OF THE KNEE IS 180 DEGREES. THE SPOONS ARE BEING FEATHERED AS THE HANDS ARE PUSHED DOWN AND AWAY. AVOID DROPPING THE WRISTS TOO FAR WHEN FEATHERING THE OARS.

SIDE VIEW OF THE CHECKPOINT TWO POSITION. THE CALF AND THIGH ANGLE ON THE INSIDE OF THE KNEE WILL BE AT APPROXIMATELY 165 DEGREES. THE SPOONS ARE FLAT.

Checkpoint three — half slide

The same principles spoken about in 'checkpoint two' apply, except that the knees have been raised and the sliding seat moved by a further 20cm (8in) to the midpoint of the runners. Your weight is on the balls of your feet, body posture is firm and upright. Stretch your arms forward. The hands and oar handles are approximately 10cm (4in) beyond your kneecaps. The oars are perpendicular to the boat and parallel to the water. The spoons are flat and rest on the water. You are now at the 'half slide position'.

Boat balance at checkpoint three

At the half slide position, apply the downward pressure of your hands on the oar handles so that the spoons are clear of the water and feathered. Your body weight is on the balls of your feet.

The following key points are worth remembering:

- Apply lateral pressure to the swivel pins.
- Distribute your weight evenly between the buttocks, hands and toes.
- Keep the upper body still. Relax!
- Avoid collecting water on the spoons.
- Your body posture is slightly forward of the vertical and your arms are fully stretched.

Checkpoint four — three-quarter slide

The major variation between checkpoints three and four is that you have raised your knees higher and that your sliding seat is now paused 60cm (24in) forward (depending on your leg length and body size). In this position the angle between your thigh and your calf below your knee should be at roughly 90 degrees; this is often referred to as the leg angle. The angle between the torso and the thigh is often called the body angle.

Keep your body posture upright, move the oar handles further forward and simultaneously raise your knees (hence the sliding seat moves forward). Pause when the oar handles are in line with and above your ankles. The spoons are feathered. You are now paused at the 'three-quarter slide position'.

Boat balance at checkpoint four

At the three-quarter slide position, continue by applying the downward pressure of your hands on the oar handles so that the spoons are clear of the water and feathered. Your body weight is on the balls of your feet. Apply force against the lateral pressure, evenly distribute your weight and keep the upper body still and relaxed. Avoid collecting water on the spoons, as this affects your stroke and boat balance.

SIDE VIEW OF THE CHECKPOINT THREE POSITION. THE WEIGHT IS ON THE BALLS OF THE FEET, ARMS STRETCHED FORWARD. THE HANDS AND OAR HANDLES HAVE EXTENDED ROUGHLY 10CM (4IN) PAST THE KNEE-CAPS. THE CALF AND THIGH ANGLE IS ABOUT 140 DEGREES.

SIDE VIEW OF THE CHECKPOINT FOUR POSITION. THE KNEES AND ANKLES ARE NOW BOTH AT ROUGHLY 90 DEGREES. THE OAR HANDLES ARE PUSHED FURTHER FORWARD AND THE SPOONS FEATHERED IN THE 'THREE-QUARTER SLIDE POSITION' IN PREPARATION FOR THE CATCH.

Checkpoint five — full slide

The transition from checkpoint four to checkpoint five can be achieved by simply lifting your knees to their fullest extent. This position is known either as the 'full slide' or the 'frontstops' position. Remember to maintain an upward body posture; with your head up, look ahead at the horizon and not at your feet! Raise the knees and simultaneously stretch your arms forward, with the oars in hand — the sliding seat will move forward automatically. The hands and oar handles are paused with your hands extended beyond the saxboards. The spoons are feathered.

Boat balance at checkpoint five

Stop the boat and assume the position described above. Square the spoons in the water and balance the boat. Lower the hands to lift the spoons approximately 5cm (2in) above the surface of the water. You are now paused at the frontstops or 'full slide catch position'. Balancing a static boat at this position is extremely challenging, but worth persevering with.

Step 1 CHECKPOINT ONE POSITION, THE BLADES SQUARED AND BURIED IN THE WATER. THE HANDS ARE IN LINE WITH THE SOLAR PLEXUS.

Step 2 THE HANDS ARE PUSHED DOWN TO THE LAP AND THEN BROUGHT BACK UP AGAIN, MAINTAINING BOAT BALANCE AND KEEPING YOUR BODY TOTALLY RELAXED. YOUR WEIGHT SHOULD BE ON YOUR FEET.

SIDE VIEW OF THE CHECKPOINT FIVE POSITION, KNOWN AS THE 'FULL SLIDE' OR 'FRONTSTOPS' POSITION. IT IS VITAL TO KEEP YOUR HEAD UP AND LOOKING AHEAD AT THE HORIZON. DO NOT LOOK DOWN AT YOUR FEET. THE HANDS AND OAR HANDLES ARE PAUSED WITH YOUR HANDS EXTENDED BEYOND THE SAXBOARDS. THE SPOONS ARE FEATHERED.

Balancing with square spoons

Step 1

Sit at checkpoint one, spoons square in the water.

Step 2

Lower the oar handles to the lap. Repeat the cycle fluidly and smoothly. Perform one cycle at a time, gradually increasing the number cycles as well as the speed of repetition. Aim to continuously lower and raise the hands and oar handles while maintaining perfect boat balance. During the movement of the hands and oar handles it is essential that you remain relaxed. Maintain an upright body posture, keeping your weight on your feet, with your legs flat and your knees close together. (This exercise is described for checkpoint two but is relevant for all the checkpoints.)

A GOOD DRILL TO PRACTISE TO IMPROVE YOUR SKILLS AND GAIN CONFIDENCE IS TO ROCK THE BOAT. YOU CAN DO THIS BY RAISING ONE HAND AND OAR HANDLE AS YOU LOWER THE OTHER. ENSURE THAT THROUGHOUT THIS DRILL THE BLADES ARE FLAT ON THE WATER.

Manoeuvring your Boat

The finer elements of controlling your boat need to be applied with a reasonable amount of practice. There are also various commands with which you need to become familiar. It is important for you to be able to recognize and respond to these commands when they are issued in a larger crew boat.

How to stop your boat

The threat of a 'collision course' naturally calls for fast reactions. As you become aware of the pending danger, someone should scream 'Ahead!', or 'Sculler!'. The corresponding command may be 'Hold it hard'. Whatever the situation, it is important that everyone is aware that you are in danger and that you need to respond and stop your boat without any delay. In other words: you've got to apply the brakes!

Gentler stopping actions are the norm, but there will be instances where the boat needs to be brought to an abrupt halt. Such instances include having to stop the boat prior to doing a specific exercise, where your coach or the coxswain wants to explain something to you beforehand, or when the boat needs to be still before a race can commence. In each of these cases the stopping procedure is similar to that which is mentioned below, except that the process does not need an urgent reaction; it can be achieved in a more deliberate, leisurely and gentle manner.

Step 1

Lift the oar handles as quickly as possible to force the semi-feathered spoons to break the water's surface, thus slowing the boat.

Step 2

The spoons are gradually squared and, as a result, the boat will come to an abrupt stop.

The fastest way to stop your boat

A quicker method of stopping your boat is to fall out. Swing one oar out to the side and roll into the water. The boat will stop very, very quickly. This is not a recommended course of action but is worth keeping in mind in the event of a dire emergency. It is easiest to achieve for a single scull, a pair boat or a double. Larger crews require greater communication in order to bring their craft to a halt in this manner.

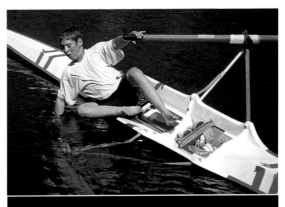

THE FASTEST WAY TO STOP YOUR BOAT IS BY SIMPLY FALLING OUT.

How to turn your boat around

Turning your boat through 180 degrees is a process that will be exercised often, and there are several ways of accomplishing the 'about turn'.

The sculling turn, with your legs straight, is important to know. Instructions for this are as follows:

Step 1

Stop the boat. Assume the checkpoint one position.

Step 2

Reverse the direction of one of the spoons (say, the right hand and arm) and submerge that spoon.

Step 3

The left hand and arm follows the movement of the active right hand and arm. The spoon remains feathered, which assists in maintaining a balanced boat.

Step 4

Once the backing action has been completed, the right spoon is feathered and supports the balance of the boat, with the left hand and arm fully stretched and the left spoon squared and submerged, so that it is covered by water.

Avoid submerging the neck or any part of the loom, the part between the oar's blade and the handle.

Draw the arm and handle to the solar plexus. Keep the left spoon submerged. This rowing action is known as 'touching the boat around'. The passive hand and arm will either lead or follow the active arm and hand, with the spoon feathered. Both arms and handles will be drawn back to the solar plexus. You should repeat these actions until you have turned the boat through 180 degrees.

An advanced version of the 'sculling turn' includes the full or partial use of your legs and sliding seat.

EXECUTING A SCULLING TURN IN A COXLESS FOUR REQUIRES A CONSIDERABLE AMOUNT OF COORDINATION AND COMMUNICATION BETWEEN THE CREW MEMBERS. FIRST THE ONE SIDE BACKS THE BOAT, THEN THE OTHER SIDE ROWS FORWARDS. AN ADVANCED VERSION OF THIS TURN INCLUDES THE USE OF YOUR LEGS AND SLIDING SEAT.

How to reverse the boat ('backing the boat down')

Step 1
Stop the boat. Adopt the checkpoint one position.

Step 2
Reverse the direction of both of the spoons at the same time, then submerge them.

Step 3
Push the oar handles forward in order to commence the backing action. The spoons remain submerged and squared while the hands and arms are extended to the

REVERSING OR 'BACKING THE BOAT DOWN' IS AN IMPORTANT SKILL, ESPECIALLY WHEN ALIGNING YOUR BOAT PRIOR TO THE START OF A RACE.

fully stretched position. Ensure that the loom of the oar does not submerge and that the spoons are covered by water. To aid extraction you should feather the top of the spoons away from yourself. To balance the boat during the recovery you can skim the spoons along the water. Repeat this action as often as required to reverse your boat to the desired position. As you become more confident you can add sliding seat movement to increase the length of each stroke.

Single-stroke rowing

From this point onwards you need to become familiar with the commands which will accompany the subsequent rowing actions. You need to respond to these commands instantly. The coxswain or a nominated crew-member issues the commands, which become increasingly important in the larger crew boats as they are intended to synchronize the actions of the crew. They also indicate each crew-member's state of readiness to proceed with whatever is required.

The 'checkpoint one' cycle

Step 1
At the command 'Backstops', sit at the backstops position, spoons flat on the water.

Step 2
After a short pause the command 'Are you ready?' will follow. Square the oars.

Step 3
Again, after a short pause, the command 'Go' or 'Row' is given.

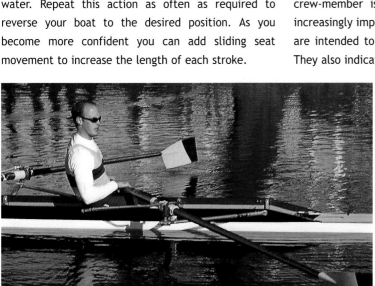

CHECKPOINT ONE POSITION IN A SWEEP-OARED BOAT. NOTE THAT THE SPOONS ARE SQUARED AND SITTING JUST ABOVE THE WATER'S SURFACE, WAITING FOR THE COMMAND TO 'GO' OR 'ROW'.

The recovery or preparation phase

- Using your hands, apply downward pressure on the oar handles. The sliding seat remains still and the spoons will rise out of the water. You simultaneously feather the spoons and push your hands away.
- The arms follow your hands smoothly to the point where they are fully stretched forward and your hands reach mid-shin, at which point your body should swing forward to the catch position.
- The knees rise fluidly and smoothly, until your sliding seat is as close to your heels as possible.
- Your legs are then fully compressed and your arms are fully stretched forward.

Step 4

The drive phase

- As the hands rise and the spoons enter the water, the full pressure of the loaded spoons will be applied to your fingers. Your body weight should be placed on your toes.
- The knees are thrust downwards as you hang on the handles, maintaining a firm upright body posture.

- The legs and knees are driven downwards until flat.
- The hands and arms maintain the momentum developed by the legs and the arms draw the handles towards the solar plexus.
- The shoulders and chest are opened. A common coaching point is that the shoulder blades should be able to squeeze a 'squash ball' or 'crack a nut'. This extension of the draw will assist in the acceleration of the oar handles towards the finish of the stroke.
- The body posture remains firm and concludes in the dining-room chair position, shoulders remaining in a horizontal plane throughout the stroke.
- The 'checkpoint one cycle' is completed as the hands commence the recovery phase and the downward pressure from the hands has released the spoons from the water. The hands and handles of the oars have returned to your lap.
- A useful command that can be given prior to pausing in this position is 'Strike'.
- Once you are able to cope with the 'checkpoint one cycle' you will then be able to follow and complete the remaining three checkpoint cycles.

SIR STEVEN REDGRAVE AND MATTHEW PINSENT DEMONSTRATING AWESOME LEG DRIVE DURING THE 1988 OLYMPIC GAMES SEMIFINAL OF THE MEN'S HEAVYWEIGHT COXLESS PAIRS IN ATLANTA, USA. THE PAIR WENT ON TO CLAIM THE GOLD MEDAL.

THE SEARLE BROTHERS AT THE CHECKPOINT ONE POSITION WHILE COMPETING IN THE MEN'S HEAVYWEIGHT COXED PAIRS AT THE 1992 BARCELONA OLYMPIC GAMES. EVEN IN A SMALL BOAT SUCH AS A PAIR, IT IS POSSIBLE TO FIT A COXSWAIN ALMOST ENTIRELY INTO THE BOWS OF THE BOAT. IN SUCH CIRCUMSTANCES THE COXSWAIN NATURALLY USES A SPEAKER SYSTEM TO RELAY COMMANDS TO THE CREW BEHIND HIM.

Multiple-stroke rowing

Having familiarized yourself with single-stroke rowing, the next logical step is to combine the single stroke cycles into continuous movement. The best start to make in continuous rowing is from the respective checkpoint positions. Start at checkpoint one and string strokes together; then move on to checkpoints two and three and try to become proficient at these points of reference before you progress to increasing the amount of knee and sliding seat movement.

You need to be patient and determined to focus your full attention on the rowing stroke cycles from these three positions as they embrace all the elements of the complete rowing stroke. Stay away from full-slide rowing in the early stages of your learning process. The most helpful exercises at this stage of your development as a rower are those where the number of strokes increases by one stroke at a time, then decreases from each respective checkpoint position.

Checkpoint one rowing

This exercise involves one stroke and strike, then two strokes and strike, then three strokes and strike ... all the way up to 10 strokes, after which you go back down the scale, reducing by one stroke at a time. The benefit derived from the exercise is that you execute multiple strokes as well as boat balance exercises all at the same time. Next, move on to checkpoint two rowing, then checkpoint three, following the same procedure for each checkpoint.

How to steer your boat straight

The first principle is to ensure that you apply an even pressure on both oars. Both spoons should be covered equally by water. Equal pressure must be maintained throughout the stroke cycle. The pressure is maintained on the spoons and both hands are drawn to an equal height in line with the solar plexus. Beware of drawing either of the oar handles towards your hip area.

Your objective is to leave successive sets of puddles in your wake, maintaining a straight line from behind the stern of the boat. The key indicator is the wash coming off the stern. You can monitor the wash throughout the entire stroke.

Before setting off on any rowing expedition, practice or race, you need to be aware of where to point the bows of the boat. First look over one shoulder, then decide on your direction, then look beyond the stern of your boat and pick out two points (one behind the other), that you will use along with your puddles to judge your straight-line progress.

STEERING ON A BUOYED RACING COURSE MAKES IT MUCH EASIER TO MAINTAIN A STRAIGHT LINE THAN ON OPEN WATER.

THIS SUCCESSION OF PUDDLES IS AMPLE EVIDENCE THAT THE SCULLER IS TRAVELLING IN A STRAIGHT LINE. SOMETIMES IT MAY BE EASIER TO SEE THE WASH COMING OFF THE STERN OF THE BOAT AND ALIGN THAT WITH STATIC REFERENCE POINTS IN THE DISTANCE.

How to turn to bowside or to strokeside

There are bound to be times when your boat drifts away from your intended course and you need to correct the boat's direction either by steering towards the bowside (your left) or towards the strokeside (your right). Fortunately, there is no need to stop rowing with both hands as you can alter the course of your boat while on the move. It is best to make adjustments immediately, rather than waiting until you are too far off course. In this instance imagine that you need to move to your right-hand (or stroke) side to correct your path (reverse the actions when you need to move to your left-hand side).

Step 1
First you need to recognize that you are beginning to row off course.

Step 2
Reduce the length and pressure on the strokeside until you are back on course.

How to dock the boat

You must be aware of the local water rules, as this can affect your approach to the jetty. Arriving back at the jetty is conducted with caution. It is a good idea to approach the jetty against the tide and wind — this will allow more control as you will not approach too fast. You should first stop at least 30m (32 yd) away from the jetty in order to check that the way ahead is clear. Having completed your observation, point the bows towards the jetty and row lightly and gently towards it. When you get to within 10m (11 yd) of the jetty you should stop rowing and let the boat drift in with the momentum you have already created. You can feather the spoon of the oar closest to the jetty while you gently stop the run of the boat with the opposite oar. You should maintain the stopping action until your boat has turned parallel to the jetty.

How to disembark from the boat

Step 1

When you have arrived alongside the jetty you should take hold of both oar handles with the hand that is furthest from the jetty. With the hand nearest to the jetty, stop the boat and prepare to disembark. Use the outside oar to turn the bows away from the jetty.

Step 2

Remove your feet from your stretcher shoes and put your feet on the slide deck.

Step 3

Stand up on the slide deck (not the hull!) and step out of the boat onto the jetty, drawing the waterside oar handle with you. Place the waterside oar across the beam of the boat.

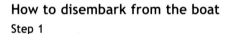

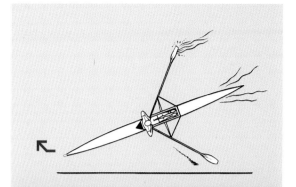

below left TURNING TOWARD THE JETTY BY DRAGGING A SQUARED BLADE ALONG THE WATER — KEEP AN EYE ON SPEED AND DISTANCE.

top WHEN APPROACHING THE DOCK YOU CAN GENTLY BRING THE BOAT TO A HALT BY PLACING THE OPPOSITE OAR LIGHTLY IN THE WATER UNTIL YOU HAVE TURNED PARALLEL TO THE JETTY. FEATHER THE SPOON OF THE JETTY-SIDE OAR.

centre PUSH THE OAR HANDLES FORWARD AND HOLD THEM TOGETHER. THE LEFT-HAND BLADE SHOULD BE FLAT ON THE WATER FOR BALANCE, WHILE THE RIGHT-HAND BLADE SHOULD CAREFULLY BE PLACED FLAT ON THE JETTY.

above PLACE THE WATERSIDE OAR ACROSS THE BEAM OF THE BOAT TO KEEP THE BOAT STABLE AGAINST THE JETTY.

Essential Techniques

Progressing towards a perfect technique requires patience and repetitive practice. However, relaxation is also essential, and you can be certain to hear the word 'relax' more often than any other during your rowing career!

The technique of the rowing and sculling strokes requires a continuous sequence of individual actions to form a single rhythmical and flowing entity. You should strive for a complete absence of 'jolts and jars'. Your whole attention should be focused on smooth and perpetual motion of your body and stroke, which should translate into a smooth path through the water.

An experienced and competent coach will lead you along the road to perfection much quicker than you could dream of on your own. He or she will focus your attention on one or two points or exercises at a time in order to extract the required results from you.

The coach has trained eyes for the job and, with the aid of a video camera, can offer you instant feedback and advice on the smallest detail in your technique. Slow-motion recall reduces each movement to microscopic proportions, giving you absolute clarity on the technical elements that need more attention.

The greater perspective of coaching encompasses many important elements of life. The coach has the prospect of making life-long friendships despite age differences. It is also about giving of him- or herself to the athletes under his or her influence; not only teaching technique, rigging and race plans, but teaching life skills as well as providing spiritual encouragement.

top STAKEBOAT STARTS. **above** BEING A COACH ENTAILS A LOT MORE THAN JUST BARKING ORDERS.

right ALL THE HOURS OF HARD WORK PAY OFF WHEN A SCULLER CAN CREATE A SMOOTH AND PERPETUAL STROKE PATH THROUGH THE WATER.

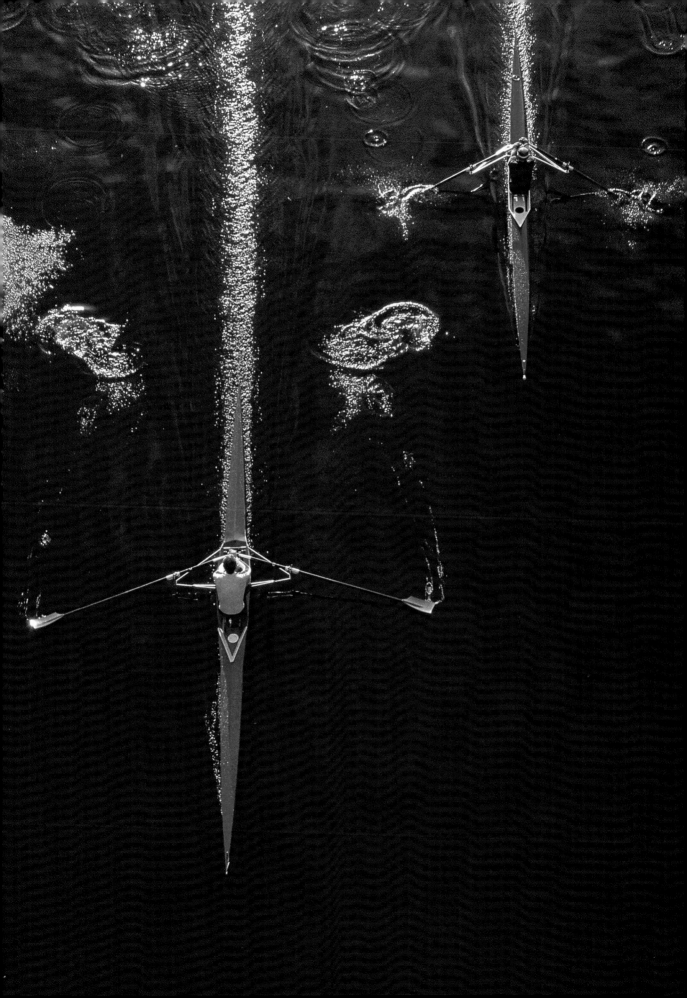

The rowing stroke

The strokes used in rowing and sculling are essentially identical, apart from a difference in the body swing angle during the arm draw. Naturally, in sculling there are two oars/spoons, but in the following description the singular will be used. Each stroke is independent and requires you to be poised, relaxed, elastic and able to apply dynamic physical power. There are two specific phases of the rowing and sculling cycle, which are known as the 'power (or drive) phase' and the 'recovery (or preparation) phase'. The applied rhythm of the stroke is subdivided on the basis of a 2:1 ratio (two parts recovery to one part drive) as follows:

Power Phase	Recovery Phase
Spoon placement	Recovery and
Leg drive	Preparation
Arm draw	Sliding seat control
Finish	The catch

Spoon placement

The stroke commences as the spoon is placed in the water. Your body posture is firm, your back, shoulders, arms and fingers remain relaxed and elastic. Your knees are lifted to your chest. The sliding seat and your buttocks are beneath your shoulders. Your body weight is poised on the balls of your feet. Your shins are vertical. The front edge of the sliding seat is as close to your heels as you can manage — you are thoroughly compressed. Don't 'bounce' into the catch with your seat — control is a key element of using the slide. Your arms and the oar handles are extended beyond the saxboards prior to the catch — really stretched out (well, more like spread-eagled!).

The arms should be approaching horizontal from the shoulders, subject to the rigging. As the connection to the water is made, the spoon cuts into the water like a 'hot knife into butter' — lightly and delicately, yet at the same time quickly.

The catch is something that you will only perfect over years of rowing. Speed is important, as is the timing of the entry and subsequent sequencing on the drive. However, it is essential that you avoid any pulling or tugging on the oar handle.

The leg drive

The leg drive commences and accelerates as you 'hang' onto the handle with your fingers while the boat is levered past the oar's point of entry to the water by the dynamic accelerating power from your legs, which after the drive have straightened out. During this phase you remain elastic and 'suspended', with your body posture remaining upright, firm and unchanged between the balls of your feet and your fingers on the oar handle. At this point the spoon is still in the water.

SPOON PLACEMENT OCCURS WITH YOUR KNEES LIFTED UP TO YOUR CHEST. THE SPOON SHOULD CUT INTO THE WATER LIKE A 'HOT KNIFE INTO BUTTER'. IT SHOULD BE GENTLE YET QUICK. AT ALL COSTS TRY TO AVOID PULLING OR TUGGING ON THE OAR.

THE LEG DRIVE STARTS AS YOU 'HANG' ONTO THE HANDLE WHILE THE BOAT IS PULLED PAST THE SPOON'S ENTRY POINT IN THE WATER DRIVEN BY THE DYNAMIC ACCELERATING POWER GENERATED BY YOUR LEGS, WHICH THEN FLATTEN OUT.

THE ARM DRAW KEEPS THE PRESSURE CONSTANT BETWEEN THE SPOON, WATER AND FOOTBOARD. THE CAVITY CREATED BEHIND THE SPOON WILL ENABLE A CLEAN EXTRACTION. THE ARM DRAW ENDS WITH THE HANDS CLOSE TO THE SOLAR PLEXUS.

EXTRACTION OF THE SPOON SIGNALS THE END OF THE DRIVE AND START OF THE RECOVERY PHASE. THE SPOON IS RELEASED FROM THE WATER BY TAPPING DOWN AND AWAY. PRESS THE HANDLE TO YOUR LAP WITH YOUR OUTSIDE HAND AND KEEP THE SPOON SQUARE.

The arm draw

The arm draw maintains a constant pressure between the spoon, the water and footboard, which is coupled with the accelerating leg action and a back swing of between 5–10 degrees in sculling and 15–20 degrees in rowing. The stroke concludes close to the solar plexus, with arms, hands and full water pressure in the back of the fingers being drawn towards the body and to the point where the spoon is released from the water by tapping down and away (see below). Bear in mind that the shoulders should travel in a horizontal plane throughout the stroke.

The recovery phase

The spoon extraction is known as the 'finish' and completes the power phase of the stroke. Chest is open, elbows are drawn back and out slightly, squeezing an imaginary squash ball between your shoulder blades. Forearms are parallel with the water.

The clean extraction of the spoon follows downward pressure from the hands upon the oar handle. As you extract the spoon from the water, you keep it 'square' by pressing the oar handle towards your lap with your outside hand (the one furthest from the spoon) when rowing. Your thumbs will most likely slightly brush against your body. In sculling, the hands should be finishing in front of the body, and not out to the side or past your body! The spoon leaves the water vertically and square and is subsequently feathered by turning the handle with your fingers (of the inside hand in rowing), keeping your wrists relatively flat in relation to the hands and forearms.

Wrist drop is a common problem in novice rowers and needs to be addressed urgently. To avoid this, remind yourself constantly that the fingers feather the oar, NOT the wrist! Body posture should be in the 'dining-room chair backrest' position, almost upright and firm. Head up and, again, look up at the treetops!

Recovery and preparation

Sit at checkpoint one — the backstops

The arms, led by the hands, flow smoothly away from the body. Hold the oar handle lightly in the fingers with your thumbs beneath the oar handle which, in turn, is cupped between your thumbs and fingers, the latter as close as comfortable to the ends of each oar handle. Lateral pressure from your thumbs and fingers on the button against the swivels is essential. All eight of your fingers will be on top of the handle, but when rowing, avoid allowing the little finger of the outside hand to hang over the end of the oar handle. At the same time you must push your hands and arms forward until they are fully stretched at the checkpoint three position, and beyond your knees which will have remained flat. Your body posture is slightly forward of the vertical and your arms and shoulders are fully stretched.

You should have the feeling that every lateral muscle, running from your hips up through your side and back muscles, and down to your fingertips, is being stretched, while the sliding seat remains stationary. Think about the important skeletal muscles for rowing which are being stretched (see pages 84–85).

The key word 'relax' must be uppermost in your mind, along with 'light hands on the oar handles' and keeping your body firm yet relaxed, your body weight evenly spread on the balls of your feet. Your body weight needs to be shifted both in the centre and towards the forward lip of the sliding seat.

It is useful to remember the three-point balance as: fingers — sliding seat — balls of the feet.

Sliding seat control

The knees commence their flexing and then are raised as the hands pass through checkpoint three. The sliding seat will move in complete harmony with the raising of the knees and the speed of the boat. Your body weight should be evenly distributed on the balls of the feet. The flowing hands continue to lead the arms towards the catch in an uninterrupted and elastic action relative to the existing striking rate.

The sliding seat reaches the frontstops without 'bouncing' and is stationary for a fraction of a second as the spoon is squared in advance of reaching checkpoint five, the catch position. The knees at this point should be at armpit height.

THE RECOVERY PROVIDES AN OPPORTUNITY TO CATCH YOUR BREATH AND PREPARE FOR THE NEXT STROKE AS THE BOAT 'RUNS' BENEATH YOU. THE FURTHER THE BOAT TRAVELS BETWEEN STROKES IN THIS WAY, THE LESS ENERGY WILL BE NEEDED TO COVER A GIVEN DISTANCE.

CONTROL OF THE SLIDING SEAT ALLOWS THE BOAT TO 'RUN' THROUGH THE WATER IN THE MOST EFFICIENT MANNER WHILE GIVING THE CREW SUFFICIENT TIME TO PREPARE FOR THE NEXT STROKE. A 'RUSHED SLIDE' CAN UPSET THE BALANCE AND REDUCE THE SPEED OF THE BOAT.

The catch

The hands move gently upwards in the final preparation for the spoon's entry and placement in the water. The arms from the shoulders should be near horizontal to the water. Once again, rigging will play a part in achieving this. The spoon is placed into the water and your full body weight is transferred onto your footboard and onto your oar handle, as you synchronize your leg drive with the spoon.

SLIDING SEAT CONTROL REQUIRES THAT THE SEAT MOVE IN HARMONY WITH THE RAISING OF THE KNEES. IT SHOULD REACH THE FRONTSTOPS WITHOUT 'BOUNCING' AND SHOULD BE STATIONARY FOR A FRACTION OF A SECOND AS THE SPOON IS SQUARED BEFORE THE CATCH.

IN THE CATCH THE SPOON IS DIPPED INTO THE WATER AS YOUR FULL BODY WEIGHT IS TRANSFERRED ONTO FOOTBOARD AND OAR HANDLE. AT THE SAME TIME YOU SHOULD TRANSFER YOUR LEG DRIVE TO THE SPOON THROUGH A FIRM TORSO AND STRAIGHT ARMS.

Technique exercises

The stroke cycle is compressed into a very small amount of time. Between 40–50 small details go into one stroke, and at a stroke rate of 30 strokes per minute (the striking rate), you are repeating the stroke action every two seconds. Depending on the type of training you are doing, the coach may have you rowing at 12 strokes to the minute (which equals one stroke every five seconds), or at 40 strokes to the minute (one stroke every 1.5 seconds). Many elite athletes have been seen to come out of the start of a race at over 50 strokes per minute.

Correct application and execution of the stroke knows no shortcuts. It is advisable to constantly refresh yourself on the correct technique, as it is so easy for a small flaw in technique to disrupt an otherwise acceptable application. The purpose of technique exercise is to enable you to selectively focus your attention on each successive activity making up the stroke cycle.

RATEMETERS CAN BE USED TO MEASURE STROKE RATE PER MINUTE. MANY COXSWAIN AMPLIFIER SYSTEMS COME EQUIPPED WITH RATEMETER FUNCTIONS. SOME COXLESS BOATS HAVE A FIXED RATEMETER SYSTEM WHICH RECORDS THE RATE FROM THE SEAT MOVEMENT.

Each exercise should be executed where it applies at the respective checkpoints one through to five, either as single or multiple strokes. It is important to isolate your actions by initially limiting the amount of sliding seat action in order to establish the exact point of breakdown in the stroke process. You will benefit by starting at checkpoint one and methodically progressing to checkpoint four (the three-quarter slide) before using the full slide.

As you progress through the stroke you will establish the point of breakdown, and if you concentrate your efforts on all the checkpoints up to four, you will be well placed to eventually execute effective full strokes.

The comfortable and 'correct' set-up of the athlete in the cockpit is vital to the success of that athlete. Rigging is an art, and small variations (some of only 2mm; 0.08in) can and do have a bearing on the ability of the athlete to achieve and maintain a reasonable technique. Correct rigging is essential in competition as well as in all training exercises.

Technique correction

The purpose of these exercises is to lead you towards perfection of rowing technique by overcoming unnecessary movements and to focus your attention on the simplest actions, ensuring they are effective and physically economical. Another essential consideration is ensuring that individual and crew interest and concentration is maintained throughout the duration of each outing.

Eyes closed

Many coaches subscribe to the practice of sharpening your technical focus and sense of concentration, balance and rhythm by including brief periods of rowing with your eyes closed; for instance, for 5–10 seconds – no longer, as you don't want to risk rowing into another craft.

Each of the following exercises should be practised with your eyes closed. This enables you to visualize every movement you make in your mind's eye.

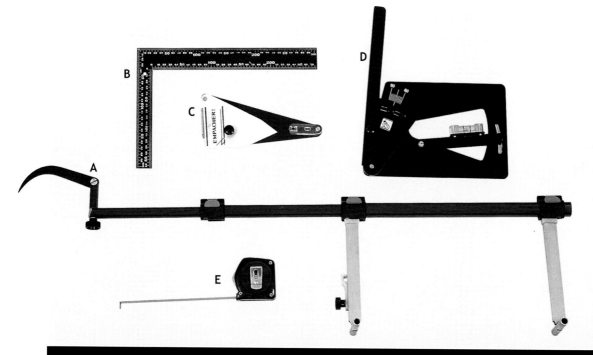

A VARIETY OF RIGGING TOOLS ARE USED TO ADJUST SETTINGS ON A BOAT. A HEIGHT STICK (A) ALLOWS QUICK COMPARISON OF SWIVEL HEIGHTS AND CAN BE MEASURED USING A SET SQUARE (B). PITCH GAUGES (C & D) CAN BE USED TO MEASURE THE STERN PITCH AND THE LATERAL PITCH, AS WELL AS THE ANGLE OF THE FOOTBOARD. A TAPE MEASURE (E) IS USED TO CALCULATE THE SPAN OF THE RIGGERS OR AN OAR'S INBOARD AND OUTBOARD LENGTHS.

Rowing with your feet out of your shoes

Rowing and sculling is like dancing — it is delicate, rhythmical and requires poise and precision. It is not a ham-handed, bull in a china shop, flat-footed business! You must be able to execute all the following exercises with your feet out of your shoes while focusing your attention on balancing on the balls of your feet.

Feet out of shoes — exercise 1

Take your feet out of your shoes and place them on top of the shoes. Sit at checkpoint one. Make sure that the balls of your feet remain in firm contact with your shoes. Your heels are raised and your toes are pointed towards your shoes. At the finish of each rowing stroke you must focus on completing the stroke at the one o'clock position (about 10 degrees). Each sculling stroke should be completed with your back upright as in the dining-room chair position. Your feet remain connected to the footboard when your legs are fully stretched and flat.

Coach's call phrase

'Keep your weight on your feet.'

Exercise procedures

■ This exercise should be carried out at the following checkpoints: 1; 1—2; 1—3; and 1—5.

■ Perform these drills first as single strokes, then as multiple strokes.

Feet out of shoes — exercise 2

Sit at one o'clock at checkpoint one at the backstop position of each rowing stroke. In a sculling boat your back is in the equivalent position to the backrest of a dining-room chair. Your weight is pressed to the footboard and your legs are fully stretched and flat. Your heels are raised and your toes are pointed towards your shoes.

Coach's call phrase

'Stretch yourself, keep your legs flat, sit still with your weight on your feet.'

Exercise procedures

■ Perform these drills as single strokes at the following checkpoints: 1; 3; 1—2; 1—3; and 1—5.

■ Perform these drills as multiple strokes at the following checkpoints: 1; 3; 1—2; 1—3; and 1—5.

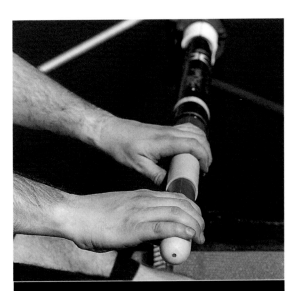

THE SWEEP-OAR GRIP WITH THE BLADE SQUARED. THE WRISTS ARE ON A FLAT PLANE WITH THE KNUCKLES AND FOREARMS. ALTHOUGH THE GRIP WITH THE FINGERS IS FIRM, THE THUMBS SHOULD BE RELAXED AS THE PITCH OF THE SPOON IS CONTROLLED BY THE SWIVEL.

THE SWEEP-OAR GRIP WITH THE BLADE FEATHERED. NOTE THE OPEN, RELAXED HANDS AND THE STRAIGHT WRISTS. ONCE THE THUMBS HAVE ROLLED THE BLADE ONTO THE FEATHER, THE SWIVEL AGAIN CONTROLS THE PITCH UNTIL THE SPOON NEEDS TO BE SQUARED ONCE MORE.

Fast hands

It is important to first appreciate that the forward movement of the hands and arms is a nonstop, smooth and continuously flowing motion. The hand speed away from the finish is the mirror image of the hand speed during the final phase of the draw and is totally relative to the striking rate at which you are working.

Fast Hands — exercise 1

Sit at checkpoint one at the backstop position of each rowing or sculling stroke. Your weight is pressed to the footboard and your legs are fully stretched and flat. Prepare and proceed to row single strokes between checkpoints one and three.

Coach's call phrase

'Get your hands away', although it is considered to be more helpful to say 'Now keep your hands flowing and stretch yourself'.

Exercise procedures

■ Perform these drills as single strokes at the following checkpoints: 1—2; 1—3; and 1—5.

■ Perform these drills as multiple strokes at the following checkpoints: 1—2; 1—3; and 1—5.

Fast Hands — exercise 2

Sit at checkpoint one and let go of your oar handle. Lift your arms and stretch them out in front of you until they are parallel with the water or the floor of the boat. Swing your arms up and down freely down to your side, up vertically, then stretched out in front of you. Do this repeatedly. Avoid any shoulder shrugging; keep your shoulders level and relaxed. Imagine sitting beneath a set of parallel bars with your shoulders in contact with the bars while moving forward on your sliding seat. Prepare and proceed to row single strokes with outstretched arms (no arm draw) between checkpoints one and three.

Coach's call phrase

'Hang on the handle and push legs down.'

Exercise procedures

■ Perform these drills as single strokes (first without arm draw, then with arm draw) at the following checkpoints: 1—2; 1—3; and 1—5.

■ Perform these drills as multiple strokes (first without arm draw, then with arm draw) at the following checkpoints: 1—2; 1—3; and 1—5.

Sculling exercise

Sculling — exercise 1

Sit still at the finish, legs and knees flat, as you commence the preparation phase. Ensure that the leading hand precedes the following hand through the crossover to checkpoint three. Exaggerate the clearance between the leading and following hands. Ensure that the following hand has space for vertical movements, then smoothly straighten your arms.

Exercise procedures

■ Single strokes (with and without arm draw) at the following checkpoints: 1—2; 1—3; 1—4; and 1—5.

■ Multiple strokes (with and without arm draw) at the following checkpoints: 1—2; 1—3; 1—4; and 1—5.

DOUBLE-SCULLING WITH YOUR COACH NOT ONLY HELPS TO ACCELERATE YOUR LEARNING CURVE, BUT ALSO ALLOWS YOU TO ATTEMPT EXERCISES IN THE KNOWLEDGE THAT THE BOAT WILL ALWAYS BE STABLE. ANOTHER BENEFIT IS THAT HANDLING THE BOAT IS MUCH EASIER WITH TWO PEOPLE.

Use of the rule of thumb in sculling

In setting yourself up for the finish in either a single, double or a quad – and when the exact entry and extraction points have not been marked up on the boat – I use what I call 'the rule of thumb' to indicate the finish position. Sit upright at checkpoint one (this applies in all types of boat) with your legs flat and the sculling oar handles drawn to your body. Point your thumbs towards one another. In the quad your thumbs should be separated by a thumb's length, in a double scull by two thumb lengths, and in a single scull by three thumb lengths.

Sweep rowing also has its own set of conventions, and these need careful attention. The standard distance between the hands on the oar handle is two hands' width. This distance will result in the outside extremities of your hands being shoulder width apart. It is important that you recognize that your inside hand alone controls the turning (squaring and feathering) of the spoon. Make certain that you cup the oar handle between the thumb and forefinger and that the oar is held comfortably by the four fingers of the hand. The role of the outside hand is limited to resting lightly on the handle during the preparation phase as well as applying the downward pressure to the handle at the finish of the stroke. This downward pressure from the outside hand extracts the spoon square and vertically.

During this exercise it is vital that lateral pressure should be maintained. Where the exact angle reference points for the finish have not been marked up on the boat, you should set the backstops position at 65cm (25in) aft of the centrepoint of the swivel pin. This will at least ensure that the entire crew is seated at the same reference point at the finish. The coach will need to set this position to take into account the height of the individual sculler.

above AT THE FINISH OR BACKSTOPS POSITION YOUR HANDS SHOULD BE ABOUT ONE-AND-A-HALF HAND WIDTHS APART. THE FOREARMS SHOULD BE HORIZONTAL AND THE WRISTS STRAIGHT AT THE FINISH.

top YOUR COACH CAN HELP YOU TO ESTABLISH THIS REFERENCE POINT.

THE CORRECT CROSSOVER OF THE HANDS IN SCULLING IS ESSENTIAL TO CREATE A BALANCED STROKE. THE KNUCKLES OF THE RIGHT HAND SHOULD BRUSH THE LEFT WRIST WHERE YOUR WATCH STRAP WOULD NORMALLY BE – FOR THIS REASON, ALWAYS REMOVE YOUR WATCH.

Adjusting the hands while rowing

Moving your inside hand on the oar

Use both hands on the handle, adjusting the inside hand in the following sequence.

Extend the inside hand outwards at full stretch towards the button; next, move the inside hand inwards (towards the handle) by approximately 20cm (8in); finally, reposition your inside hand so that it is separated from your outside hand by about 50cm (20in).

Rowing with one hand

These exercises will help you to:

- Achieve correct body posture throughout the stroke.
- Exercise control with the turning hand.
- Achieve good lateral pressure in the complete execution of the outside shoulder.

Single-hand rowing — inside hand only

Sitting at checkpoint one with outstretched arms in a sweep-oar boat, we will use 'one-hand rowing' with the inside hand, which is the turning hand. Place your inside hand in the middle of the oar handle and the outside hand on your hip. Alternate between square spoon rowing and conventional rowing, avoiding dropping the wrist at the finish and ensure that the spoon leaves the water cleanly. Continue to feel the pressure of the water in the back of your fingers.

Exercise procedures

- Perform these drills as single strokes (with and without arm draw) at the following checkpoints: 1–2; 1–3; 1–4; and 1–5.
- Perform these drills as multiple strokes (with and without arm draw) at the following checkpoints: 1–2; 1–3; 1–4; and 1–5.

Single-hand rowing — outside hand only

Place the outside hand at the end of the oar handle with your inside hand placed on your hip. The centre of attention is on the lightness of touch by the outside hand. Adopt square spoon rowing for this exercise, but aside from that you can follow the same routine as discussed in the example above.

ROWING WITH THE INSIDE HAND (OUTSIDE HAND BEHIND THE BACK). THIS EXERCISE CONCENTRATES ON THE SQUARING AND FEATHERING ACTION, CONTROLLED BY THE INSIDE HAND. THE OUTSIDE HAND PROVIDES THE PULLING POWER, SO THE EXERCISE IS PERFORMED SLOWER THAN USUAL.

Single-hand rowing — outside hand rotation

This exercise works on physical arm strength as well as timing and technique. The outside hand leaves the oar handle immediately after the entry of the spoon to the water; then the hand rises and rotates in a clockwise direction. The hand meets the oar handle in time to make the extraction by applying downward pressure to the oar handle. The outside hand rests on the handle until the beginning of the following stroke is made.

The second phase of the exercise is to execute an anti-clockwise rotation. The outside hand leaves the oar handle after the spoon extraction, and the arm rotates down towards the water. The arm swings backwards and overhead to coincide with the connection of the following stroke. The third phase of this routine is to continue rowing without any arm/hand rotation, during which time the ultra lightness of the outside hand upon the oar handle will become apparent to you.

Exercise procedures

■ Proceed with this arm rotational exercise at the following checkpoints for 10 continuous rotations in each direction: 1; 2; 3; 4; and 5.

■ Row without arm rotation with ultra light hand pressure at checkpoints: 1; 2; 3; 4; and 5.

Square spoon rowing can also be included in this routine but ensure that the spoon leaves the water cleanly at the finish and continue to feel the pressure of the water in the back of your fingers.

Single-hand rowing — outside hand on your head

Row with the inside hand on your oar handle and the outside hand on your head.

ROWING WITH THE INSIDE HAND (OUTSIDE HAND ON THE HEAD). CONCENTRATE ON CLEAN PLACEMENT AND EXTRACTION OF THE SPOON, ALLOWING IT TO FIND ITS NATURAL DEPTH IN THE WATER. THE OUTSIDE HAND WOULD NORMALLY ALSO CONTROL BLADE HEIGHT DURING THE RECOVERY.

Single-hand rowing — outside hand behind your back
Row with the inside hand on your oar handle and the outside hand placed behind you in the small of your back. Concentrate on maintaining the dining-room chair position.

Single-hand rowing — inside hand variations
Keep hold of the rigger backstay with the inside hand, at the point at which it is secured to the saxboard. Row using only your outside hand through the entire stroke cycle at the following checkpoint positions. Another version of this exercise is to row with the inside hand down the loom.

Exercise procedures
■ This exercise should be carried out at the following checkpoints: 1; 1—2; 1—3; and 1—5.
■ Perform these drills first as single strokes, then as multiple strokes.

■ Repeat this exercise as single strokes with no arm draw, then with arm draw.
■ Finally, row multiple strokes (with and without arm draw) at checkpoints: 1—2; 1—3; 1—4; and 1—5.

Square spoon exercises
Square spoon — exercise 1
Alternate between square spoon and standard sculling. The focus is initially on your ability to maintain button pressure by using your thumb to exert lateral pressure. The forefinger meets the thumb at the end of the handle, with the oar handles held by your fingers.

The lateral pressure needs to be maintained throughout the stroke, and particularly at the finish when the temptation exists to pull the hands towards each other. The exercise can first be carried out from the respective checkpoints, then as single strokes, finally moving onto multiple strokes.

ROWING WITH THE INSIDE HAND DOWN THE LOOM (top) AND THE INSIDE HAND ON THE SAXBOARD (above).

Exercise procedures

- Single strokes (with and without arm draw) at the following checkpoints: 1–2; 1–3; 1–4; and 1–5.
- Multiple strokes (with and without arm draw) at the following checkpoints: 1–2; 1–3; 1–4; and 1–5.

Square spoon – exercise 2

Alternate between square spoon rowing and the normal feathering and squaring cycle during the recovery. The focus is initially on your ability to maintain button (or outward) pressure by using your fingers and thumbs to exert lateral force. This lateral pressure needs to be maintained throughout the entire stroke cycle, in particular at the finish when there might be the temptation to release the outward pressure of the hands.

Ensure that you are seated properly at the finish, as body posture is always important. Make sure that you are sitting erect and at all times avoid slouching. Hold your head up straight. Many coaches call 'Chin up – look up' to their crews at this point. Your shoulders are square and you should maintain a three-point balance: your weight should be distributed equally on the balls of your feet as you sit on the bones of your buttocks, while your hands rest lightly on the oar handle.

Exercise procedures

- Single strokes (with and without arm draw) at the following checkpoints: 1–2; 1–3; 1–4; and 1–5.
- Multiple strokes (with and without arm draw) at the following checkpoints: 1–2; 1–3; 1–4; and 1–5.

DURING NORMAL FEATHERED SPOON ROWING AVOID THE TENDENCY TO DROP YOUR HANDS TOO FAR, AS THIS WILL UPSET THE BALANCE AND CAUSE THE BLADE TO 'SKY' AT THE CATCH.

IN SQUARE SPOON ROWING THE HANDS MUST MOVE DOWN AND AWAY FROM YOU QUICKLY IN ORDER TO CLEAR THE WATER DURING THE RECOVERY.

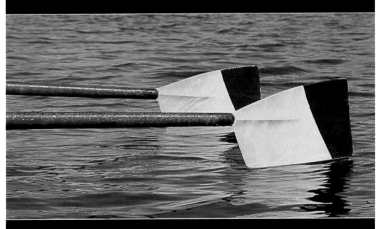

AS YOU APPROACH THE CATCH, YOUR HANDS SHOULD RISE TO BRING THE SPOON DOWN TOWARDS THE WATER'S SURFACE AN INSTANT BEFORE THE CATCH. TAKE CARE NOT TO BURY THE SPOON TOO DEEP AS THIS WILL UPSET THE BALANCE OF THE BOAT.

A USA MEN'S EIGHT DEMONSTRATING GOOD UNIFORMITY IN BLADE HEIGHT HAVING 'SQUARED' EARLY BEFORE THE CATCH.

Square spoon – exercise 3

Square spoon rowing is probably the best technique to use. Be aware of your hand height position at the catch. A good reference point is that the hand height is equal to the knee height. Place the spoon in the water cleanly at the catch and feel the pressure of the water in the back of your fingers. As you feel this pressure build, squeeze the legs downwards. Only just cover the spoon with water. Avoid rushing at the beginning and aggressively 'banging the spoon' into the water – instead, slip the spoon into the water like a hot knife into butter.

Exercise procedures

- Single strokes (with and without arm draw) at the following checkpoints: 1–2; 1–3; 1–4; and 1–5.
- Multiple strokes (with and without arm draw) at the following checkpoints: 1–2; 1–3; 1–4; and 1–5.

Square spoon – exercise 4

Square spoon rowing is again very appropriate to help overcome the breakdown of the stroke due to incorrect blade height, especially at the finish. Be aware of your hand height position at the finish, and remember that you can use the solar plexus as a reference point for your hand height. Use light hands on the oar handles at the finish and ensure that the spoon leaves the water cleanly. Continue to feel the pressure of the water in the back of your fingers.

In sculling boats, make certain that the hands and fingers are drawn upwards towards the solar plexus and that both handles are at an equal height to one another at the finish.

A common flaw is to draw the right hand downwards the right hip at the finish.

In sweep oar boats the finish must be drawn out in the same manner as for sculling. A common flaw here is to draw the handle down into the lap at the finish. This flaw will result in an ineffective finish, causing the stroke to be 'washed out', which means that the spoon has been prematurely disconnected from the water. As a result, the shortened stroke will adversely affect the boat balance and the steering of the boat will also be affected.

Exercise procedures

- Single strokes (with and without arm draw) at the following checkpoints: 1–2; 1–3; 1–4; and 1–5.
- Multiple strokes (with and without arm draw) at the following checkpoints: 1–2; 1–3; 1–4; and 1–5.

Sharpening the catch

An overview

Placing the spoon in the water at the commencement of the propulsive phase is crucial. I have used the phrase 'place the spoon' to highlight the fact that 'the beginning' (or 'the entry') is a movement of precision. Elsewhere, we have described the entry of the spoon into the water as simulating a hot knife slicing into butter. There are several exercises that can help the speed and application of 'the beginning'.

Sharpening the catch – exercise 1

Reverse your hand grip on the rowing oar handle. Stretch the hands and arms to their fullest extent. This exercise should be executed at checkpoints three, four and five. Turn your hands so that your palms face the underside of the oar handle with your thumbs cupping the top of the handle. Simultaneously raise your knees so as to achieve the checkpoint position you intend to use for the exercise.

Once you have completed this preparation phase, allow the sliding seat to be held absolutely still (fix the slide with your knees raised) as you lift the oar handle up and around the turn, with your upturned hands in an elliptical movement in order to effect the catch. Commence the process by describing the applications of the catch, then gradually increase the tempo.

Repeat this action while ensuring that the spoon is properly squared.

Your arms remain firmly stretched and elastic out in front of you. There is no leg drive or drawing and flexing of the arms during this exercise.

Sharpening the catch – exercise 2

Use a conventional handgrip and follow the same process described in exercise 1.

Sharpening the catch – exercise 3

Half and three-quarter slide rowing at checkpoints three to one and four to one. Use a conventional hand grip and follow the same process as discussed above. Gradually increase the stroke rate of application.

Adopt both square spoons as well as the conventional spoon application techniques.

THE MODERN RIGGING CONVENTION OF FOURS PLACES THE BOW AND STROKE POSITIONS ON THE SAME SIDE TO REDUCE THE TURNING EFFECT AND KEEP THE BOAT STRAIGHT. DUE TO THE PROXIMITY, ON THE SAME SIDE, OF THE NUMBER TWO AND THREE SPOONS, IT IS VITAL THAT THEY MOVE IN PERFECT HARMONY. THE FOUR ABOVE IS AT THE HALF-SLIDE POSITION AND WILL BEGIN TO SQUARE THEIR BLADES ALL THE WAY TO THE CATCH.

Coxing and steering
Coxswain: the extra body in the boat

The art and skill of coxing was brought about by the necessity for boats of different sorts having to negotiate and navigate unfamiliar, sometimes hostile and sometimes narrow waterways. So it was that, when it came to boat racing, the coxswain became an integral part of the crew – the ninth person in an eight, the fifth person in a coxed four, or the third person in a coxed pair. You may, of course, want to be the coxswain, whose job it is to steer the boat, take charge of the crew, as well as act with all the authority of the coach. The coxswain (or 'cox') is usually seated in the stern of an eight, but can be found lying back in the bows of a quad, coxed pair, or a coxed four, from where he or she steers the boat.

As a coxswain you are an integral part of the rowing crew and have the principal responsibility of assisting the coach in the preparation of the crew. You are the onboard eyes and ears of the coach and will contribute significantly to the performance of your crew.

Naturally, the less weight the crew has to carry the faster they can go, so the coxswain is normally small in

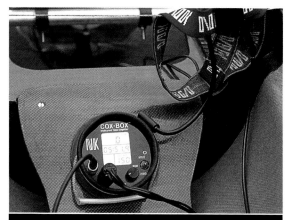

AN EXAMPLE OF THE ELECTRONIC EQUIPMENT USED BY A COXSWAIN TO AMPLIFY THE INSTRUCTIONS GIVEN THROUGH A MICROPHONE AND SPEAKER SYSTEM. THESE SYSTEMS OFTEN INCLUDE OTHER FUNCTIONS SUCH AS STROKE RATE METER, TIMER AND STROKE COUNTER.

THE CAMBRIDGE COXSWAIN CELEBRATES VICTORY OVER OXFORD IN THE ANNUAL BOAT RACE. NOTE THE CAMERA MOUNTED BEHIND THE COX FOR LIVE COVERAGE DURING THE RACE.

stature. Ideally, the junior coxswain will have a body mass of 45kg (99 lb) and the senior coxswain a body mass of 55kg (122 lb). The coxswain's role assumes massive importance in races such as the Oxford and Cambridge boat race, as well as other long distance open river events like the Head of the River for eights on the River Thames or the Head of the Charles in Boston, USA.

Imagine steering one of the two famous boat-race crews of eight oared boats ('eights') – each boat has oars with a mass of 100kg (220 lb) and carries a crew with a total mass between 640kg (1410 lb) and 800kg (1765 lb). It is a position of great power and huge responsibility. The coxswain's role is to control the burly rowers and the combined mass of almost one ton of manpower and equipment. Picture yourself seated facing your crew and racing alongside your opposition with the outcome of the race hanging in your hands.

As the cox and ninth member of the crew of eight you need to have nerves of steel, have your wits about you and, essentially, have the absolute faith of your crew-members as you attempt to out-manoeuvre and out-steer your opponents.

And all this without allowing the overlapping oars of the two crews to upset you or your crew. You have to stay within the limits of the rules as you take every possible advantage of tide and weather conditions. In a contest like this, the cox can rise to being the hero or heroine of the day.

The best coxes are fiercely competitive and intelligent racing tacticians. Far removed from the truth is the widely held opinion that the cox is on board to shout repetitive, empty comments like 'in, out, in, out'. If this were true it would drive a crew daft and any seriously competitive crew would do without a cox in favour of a lighter boat.

The cox needs to pay extreme attention to the crew as well as to the surroundings in which the crew are rowing. The cox's responsibilities include that of the crew safety: a watchful lookout is kept for other craft using the same stretch of water, and care for the boat itself is required. From the coaching perspective, you will need to communicate clearly with each rower in the boat; when you are part of an 'eight' crew you will find yourself some 15m (16yd) away from the person in the bow seat. You have an onboard electronic speaker system to assist you with your communication with your crew-members, thus enabling the crew to hear every word you say and ensuring that they respond to your information. This naturally sharpens their focus on the specifics of their technique, as well as on becoming a finely drilled unit.

The cox will strive to ensure that the crew is drilled in precision timing and togetherness, coupled with perfection in their application of power and rhythm. Today's coxswain has the assistance of an array of electronic equipment, all of which measures boat speed, elapsed time, split times for various work pieces and striking rates (or cadence — the number of strokes per minute). All this information can be downloaded onto a computer for analysis and diagnosis. During a crew's training outing the cox will note information about the crew's performance during particular work pieces and then report back to the coach and crew at the end of the outing.

In certain countries junior rowers are introduced to a quad sculling craft which is modified to cater for a coxswain. The purpose is associated with the safety of the crew in that a coxswain most certainly assists the younger children in the age group 14—16, who are naturally less experienced on the water. The crew can get on with the business of sculling while the coxes get on with their particular job of steering and keeping their eyes open for other water users or hazards.

The most common coxing commands

Commands are issued by the coach and/or, in the case of larger crew boats, the coxswain or a nominated crew-member. Usually the person in charge will outline the upcoming activity to be focused upon and then the commands follow. Basic commands are listed here.

Backstops See checkpoint one
Frontstops / Come forward See checkpoint five
Quarter-slide rowing See checkpoint two
Half-slide rowing See checkpoint three
Three-quarter slide rowing See checkpoint four
Are you ready? Asked prior to any action about to take place or any instruction about to be given. A distinct pause will exist between the 'Are you ready?' and the full instruction of the intended work piece or exercise. Another pause is included, followed by the command '**Go**' or **Row**. The usual command to stop is '**Easy**'.

THE SPEAKER SYSTEM. USED TO RELAY INSTRUCTIONS TO CREWS. THIS IS ESPECIALLY USEFUL IN EIGHTS AND BOW COXED BOATS.

Training for Rowing

Have fun and enjoy

There is a business saying that suggests that 'If you're not in business for fun and profit, then what are you doing it for?' To this could be added that 'If you're not in rowing for fun and more fun, then what are you doing it for?' The most fundamentally good reason for rowing is to do exactly that — enjoy it. When this spirit goes missing, then it's time to quit!

You need to first decide what you want out of the sport. Is it to be a recreational activity? Do you think you want to get semi-serious? Or is it to attain the top-most levels of achievement? Conservation of time and expense, study pressure, domestic pressures and the limitations placed on you by your profession are all matters which have to be considered in your decision.

There is another reality that will seriously limit your possible achievements as a rower — your own physiological potential. Despite our best efforts, trying to emulate the incredible feats of the British coxless four winners of the Sydney Olympic Games gold medal — and particularly the five consecutive Olympic golds of Sir Steven Redgrave — can only lead to frustration for the majority of rowers. There are so many heroes like Rob Waddell, Perti Karppinen, the Australian 'Awesome Foursome', and heroines like Silken Laumann and the Pair of Marnie McBean and Kathleen Heddle. They are all wonderful role models, but it is simply not possible for each one of us to rise to the heights of these talented athletes. However, the one thing all of us can do is to have as much fun as they do!

top THIS 'MOVING HEAD' ERGOMETER ATTEMPTS TO SIMULATE THE MOVEMENT AND INERTIA OF THE BOAT AND ROWER RELATIVE TO EACH OTHER.

above SIR STEVEN REDGRAVE ROWING AT TWO IN THE GREAT BRITAIN COXLESS FOUR. HIS FORMER PAIRS PARTNER, MATTHEW PINSENT, IS THE STROKE.

right A FEMALE QUAD SCULL CREW GENERATING AWESOME POWER AS THE BOW ROWER GLANCES OVER HER SHOULDER TO CHECK THEIR COURSE.

AFTER YEARS OF TRAINING AND GUT-WRENCHING EFFORT, NOTHING TASTES SWEETER THAN VICTORY. THE CELEBRATIONS FOR THE ITALIAN PAIR OF LEONARDO PETTINARI AND CARLO GADDI AT THE 1994 WORLD CHAMP'S ARE IN KEEPING WITH THEIR SENSE OF TEAMWORK — BEAUTIFULLY SYNCHRONIZED.

Where do you fit in?

Status classifications for men and women are decided according to levels of competition accomplishment, as well as the age of athletes. The International Rowing Federation, FISA (Fédération Internationale des Sociétés d'Aviron), controls international racing classifications, while each individual country's rowing federation tailors racing categories according to their own domestic requirements.

There are separate levels for men and women, and you can judge for yourself at which level you are most likely to enter the rowing status ladder.

Juniors is the first level, with age-group subdivisions from Under-13 to the Open Junior level, presently Under-18. Under-23 (U23) is the next level, and it is known by FISA as the Senior B level. The Open level follows on from the Over-23 age group. Domestic categories covering U23 and Open rowing exist and status steps are taken by athletes in accordance with the competence they have displayed in competition.

Status level

The status levels generally run along the lines of a system of upward progression, which commences with a so-called 'Senior D' level designed for newcomers to the sport. The athlete then progresses through the ranks to the 'Senior C' and then 'Senior B' levels and, finally, to the 'Senior A' level, or its equivalent level in your particular part of the world.

In general rowers and/or scullers move from one rung to the next according to the number of points they accumulate for winning events in their respective boat classes, with each success earning them points.

National systems may provide for a status system similar in concept to the following: one point is allocated to each member of a crew (a crew can also refer to a single sculler) for a win in a particular boat class. Four accumulated points may be the requisite number of points required to move the rower from the D division to the C division. An accumulated total of eight points may then be required to move up a rung to the B division, and an accumulated 12 points are required to move up to the A division. An Open Junior rower normally enters the status ladder at the domestic or club category Senior B level. Master's rowing exists for men and women who have attained the age of 27 and for whom fierce domestic and international competition continues to drive them to compete for as long as they are able to enjoy the sport. The FISA World Masters regatta is the annual world gathering of Masters from around the globe, where between 4000 and 6000 rowers meet every year to rekindle the spirit of the family of rowing. The annual regatta is held on a rotational basis at any of the world's top regatta venues.

Competition for Masters exists in eight average 'age of crew' categories. The age groups are initially split by nine years between category A (average age 27) and B (average age 36). Seven years separate category B and C (average age 43) as well as category C and D (average age 50). A five-year gap separates the remaining categories: E − average age 55; F − average age 60; G − average age 65; H average age 70.

Many international and other top athletes, who by virtue of age qualify to row as Masters, refrain from competing at this level, opting instead to continue to compete at the Open level. Many of these athletes continue to compete at the highest possible level well into their late thirties or early forties.

Training plans

Now you have an idea as to where you stand on the status ladder, you can also make the judgement of just how much time you have to spare and how much you want to and can devote to rowing?

The components of the process of development can be likened to building up a multi-layered cake. Just as the multi-layered cake rises from its base, so does your process of athletic development rise.

The base layer of our cake is technique. You will never stop trying to perfect your technique, no matter how long you continue to row. The second layer of the cake is physical fitness, flexibility and mobility. Layer three is physical strength, speed and endurance.

To achieve great heights of international and, ultimately, Olympic competition, two additional layers are needed to underpin the other three layers already mentioned: physiological attributes, as well as psychological and motivational approaches. The importance of the psychological and motivational components can never be overemphasized as these two factors of performance go under disguises such as 'killer instinct', 'the will to win', and so on.

As you develop your skill, fitness and strength base, so you will rely more and more on your own levels of guts and determination. At the top level, everyone who makes an Olympic or World Championship final has a chance of winning the gold medal. What separates the winners from the rest is their dedication to preparation and training, in addition to a sheer determination and steadfast will to win.

The following guidelines and notes provide an overview of the specific focus required at each stage of the development cycle. It is possible to compress the time scales that are outlined and, in so doing, fast-track the maturity of athletes. The fast-tracking of such people will, nevertheless, demand considerable time, dedication and commitment. A conservative stance − one which is appropriate to the majority of rowers − is adopted in the outline that follows.

THE TENSION IN THIS SCULLER'S BODY IS REFLECTED IN THE STRAIN ON HIS FACE AS HE BEGINS THE ARM DRAW OF YET ANOTHER STROKE.

SQUATS ARE AN EXCELLENT EXERCISE FOR IMPROVING YOUR LEG DRIVE. A HIGH NUMBER OF REPETITIONS HOLDING A LIGHT WEIGHT WILL IMPROVE STAMINA FOR LONG-DISTANCE RACES. A LOW NUMBER OF REPETITIONS HOLDING HEAVIER WEIGHTS WILL IMPROVE POWER DURING RACE STARTS. DON'T LIFT THE WEIGHTS WITH YOUR ARMS — THEY SHOULD REMAIN 'ON YOUR SHOULDERS' THROUGHOUT THE SQUAT.

STANDING BENCH PULLS (WITH THE BACK AND LEGS STRAIGHT THROUGHOUT) WILL HELP TO IMPROVE YOUR ARM DRAW, ESPECIALLY IF YOU TEND TO DRAW INTO YOUR LAP AND "WASH OUT".

Years 1 & 2
Technique and basic training

During your first two years of rowing you need to focus on spending time in the boat, coupled with a considerable amount of time on the ergometer. You will need to enhance your development by ensuring the soundest possible technical foundation. You will soon discover that the development of your technique is a never-ending process.

At the Under-13 and 14 age-group levels, as well as the Senior D level, the formation of your technique is of utmost importance, and thus the coaching component during this phase is vital.

Years 3 & 4
Advanced training stage

Early introduction of junior rowers to flexibility routines is as necessary as is the continuing development of the technical foundation of the Under-15 and Under-16 age group. The development process for 'Senior C' rowers — who, from experience, are usually students — can receive more robust and challenging treatment, and no harm is served by incorporating weight-training into their routines.

Once the technical foundation has been formed, you can move on to adding physical fitness and flexibility activities to the ingredients. This is your introduction to a formal training programme, most of which can be included as standard in the boat-training classes and ergometer training.

Year 5 and onwards

Time to put it all together

Training in the boat naturally builds up a lot of relevant strength but, inevitably, the day dawns when weight training must be added to the training routine. The period from year five onwards should, in general terms, be the real start of the high performance stage of your development, unless you managed to get to that level already in year four!

In year five it will be time to put all the elements together. You should be spending 16 to 20 hours a week in your training combining technique, physical fitness, flexibility, physical strength, speed and endurance, in addition to your continuing psychological and motivational preparation.

Weight training for teenagers can be included from about the age of 16, and it is important to remember that, at that age, the body is still willowy and in its essential development and growth phase. At this tender age the first imperative is that there should be careful monitoring of the weight-handling technique.

IT IS VITAL THAT YOU ALWAYS PERFORM STRETCHING EXERCISES BEFORE COMMENCING ANY FITNESS SESSION OR STRENGTH ROUTINE. STRETCHING WILL NOT ONLY HELP PREVENT INJURY TO YOUR MUSCLES, IT ALSO HELPS TO IMPROVE YOUR OVERALL MOBILITY AND FLEXIBILITY.

The introduction of weights and all the activities surrounding their use should be carefully monitored prior to introducing a full-scale weight-training regime.

Weights and bar bells are dangerous. Make sure you have an experienced coach to guide you in your technique and workload and always work with a group of three to four people of your own age group. Working with people of your own age will ensure that you don't stress your body by trying to match the workload of athletes who are older and more physically developed.

Body mass limits

Two body mass categories exist for Senior A and International category men and women athletes: the crew's average mass and the maximum individual mass.

	Crew average mass	Maximum individual mass
Lightweight		
— Men	70kg (155 lb)	72.5kg (160 lb)
— Women	57kg (125 lb)	59kg (130 lb)
Heavyweights	No mass limit	No mass limit

Coxswains of junior crews must weigh at least 50kg (110 lb), whereas all other coxswains must weigh 55kg (120 lb). Coxswains may carry a maximum dead weight of no more than 10 kg (22 lb) to achieve the all-up racing body mass.

The training year

The training year (adapted from the FISA coaching and development course), or periodization, is the buzzword for outlining the training plan, also referred to as the rowing year. When it comes to planning the international segment of an annual plan one needs to coincide one's plans with the Northern Hemisphere, where the majority of the international season is staged. The international programme overlaps with the domestic season in the north, while in the Southern Hemisphere you will find yourself having to train during the winter months and then having to undertake quite extensive rowing tours to Europe.

IT DOESN'T MATTER HOW MUCH TIME YOU SPEND IN THE GYM, HOW MANY BOOKS YOU READ OR HOW MUCH YOU KNOW — TO ROW WELL YOU NEED TO RACK UP RIVER MILES. THAT IS THE ONE WAY YOU CAN BE SURE THAT YOUR EFFORTS WILL BE REWARDED ... ALONG WITH A BALANCED TRAINING ROUTINE.

Training for rowing

The intention of what follows is to introduce you to the principles and concepts of training for rowing. This book is addressed specifically to a newcomer to the sport, either a Junior or someone who has taken up the sport a little later in life. Regardless of your age or level of attainment, you will want a smattering of information on scientific training.

You will need to rationalize for yourself your reasons for undertaking each of the supplementary training steps and to understand the process as well as the anticipated effect. Each component of the training programme needs to be understood for its purpose as well as its end result, be it the endurance aspects or the need for flexibility or strength. Along with these facets you need to take into account the degree of the specific focus of the training as it relates to you personally and your own desires and goals in the sport.

Training dosage — No pain no gain!

Individual training needs to be carefully selected and monitored. All well-planned training programmes focus on progressive increments of load in order to aid the gathering of strength and endurance as well as to develop your ability to cope with the increased levels of physical and emotional stress demanded by rowing. Your system will gradually respond to the rigours of repeated physical activity and, in the process of this adaptation, the body will make the necessary compensations from the new messages that it receives.

The principle of progressive load

By progressively increasing your training session workload you will improve your overall ability to sustain higher levels of output for increasing periods of time. There is a simple test you can perform to gauge your current capacity. If the coach instructs you to do 300 squats, but you had never achieved that amount of squats at any time in the past, you could be forgiven for stopping after, say, 100 repetitions. However, if the coach said to you 'I want you to be able to do 300 squat repetitions in 15 days' time', then your efforts would, more than likely, be a lot more positive. You can employ the progressive system to good advantage. For instance, start with 25 repetitions on day one and add 15 repetitions each day. By the due date ('in 15 days' time') you would be able to accomplish the 300 squats. Try it for yourself and see how the steady progressive increments of load actually works.

Change is as vital as rest, particularly when you are fatigued from competition and travel. Rest is the singlemost important ingredient to ensure that you can cope and improve with each session. It is important to interlace workdays with restdays so that you don't continuously overload your system. You must recognize the folly of slipping in additional work pieces simply because you think it will give you an advantage. More often than not strenuous and unrealistic activity of this type will result in you detrimentally affecting your health and, as a result, impeding your progress.

Constant adaptability

I recently heard a cricket commentator refer to what he termed 'muscle memory'. I thought this term to be very appropriate to the result that is achieved from the constant training, programming and application of a routine to the respective muscle groups to enable them to perform a specific action. All training should be designed to bring about individual adaptability to new senses, skills and actions, coupled with relative physical loads, in the hope of creating a favourable result: dancing for dancers and ballskills for hockey, cricket, soccer and rugby players.

In truth, where technique is being taught, it is imperative that attention to the individual's initial set-up has been carefully prepared. This attention to detail commences with the rigging of the boat and the application of the stroke cycle, together with the preparation and carrying out of a movement with or without weights, plus instruction on how to breathe and so on.

When you stop training, a reverse action immediately takes place — and in double-quick time. This means that a process of 'unlearning' occurs at more than twice the speed of learning. This is a problem that all athletes will encounter when they suffer from injuries that force them out of training and exercising for certain periods of time.

Be careful and sensible about your training. 'Train, don't strain' is a wise dictum to follow, along with listening to the advice of your coach.

In addition, don't be tempted to double the doses of your workload or practice in the simplistic hope of 'putting one over' on the competition. There are no shortcuts, only diligent application.

THERE'S NOTHING LIKE A ROWING CAMP TO BRING OUT THAT EDGE OF COMPETITIVENESS NEEDED TO SPUR YOU ON TO GREATER EFFORTS. CAMPS ALLOW YOU TO LEARN FROM OTHERS AS WELL AS ENJOY 'UNOFFICIAL' RACE COMPETITION. THEY ALSO ADD A BREATH OF FRESH AIR TO YOUR TRAINING YEAR.

What is included in a training programme?

We have already discussed the basic content of the training programme — now it is time to look at the specifics. Rowing is a strength and endurance sport, and respectively the water and gym programmes will take these specific needs into account. The rowing stroke is repeated 2000 or more times in a single outing, and approximately 240 times in a 2000m (2180 yd) race. The Oxford and Cambridge crews will execute about 700 strokes during their boat race.

Some basic physiology

The continuous repetition of the rowing stroke requires a consistent blood supply to all the muscle groups used in the rowing cycle. Among the objectives of rowing training is to increase the number of capillaries surrounding a muscle or group of muscles. The biological term used for ensuring enough blood-flow to the muscle is 'capillarization of the arteries'. The rowing action is in itself the best and most effective means of bringing about this development and, as a result, time in the boat or on the ergometer is of major value to your development.

Aerobic capacity

Maximal oxygen uptake (VO_2 Max) is the body's maximal aerobic power and is defined as the highest oxygen uptake the individual can attain during physical work, breathing air at sea level (Astrand, 1970). An evaluation of an athlete's VO_2 Max is the best criterion of his status of aerobic efficiency that, through training, may achieve an improvement of a maximum of between 15% and 20%.

(Frank W Dick — Sports Training Principles)

Aerobic system

Rowing races over a distance of 2000m (2180 yd) fall within the category of strength endurance sports. In other words, the aerobic system is fundamental to rowing performance and, therefore, calls upon a sound preparation of the system in order to cope with high demands of physiological output as well as the sustained application of physical strength during a race. The demands of racing are sometimes exacerbated by adverse tidal conditions and headwinds when the race, normally scheduled to take six minutes, can turn into a 10-minute horror event!

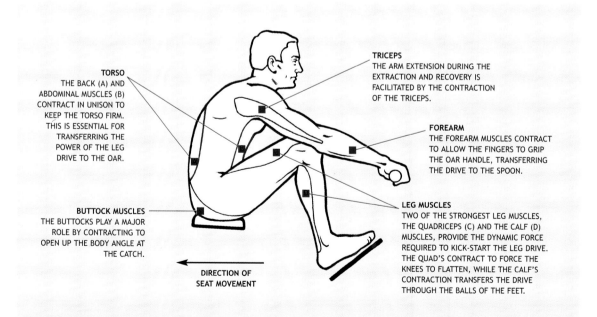

TORSO
THE BACK (A) AND ABDOMINAL MUSCLES (B) CONTRACT IN UNISON TO KEEP THE TORSO FIRM. THIS IS ESSENTIAL FOR TRANSFERRING THE POWER OF THE LEG DRIVE TO THE OAR.

TRICEPS
THE ARM EXTENSION DURING THE EXTRACTION AND RECOVERY IS FACILITATED BY THE CONTRACTION OF THE TRICEPS.

FOREARM
THE FOREARM MUSCLES CONTRACT TO ALLOW THE FINGERS TO GRIP THE OAR HANDLE, TRANSFERRING THE DRIVE TO THE SPOON.

BUTTOCK MUSCLES
THE BUTTOCKS PLAY A MAJOR ROLE BY CONTRACTING TO OPEN UP THE BODY ANGLE AT THE CATCH.

LEG MUSCLES
TWO OF THE STRONGEST LEG MUSCLES, THE QUADRICEPS (C) AND THE CALF (D) MUSCLES, PROVIDE THE DYNAMIC FORCE REQUIRED TO KICK-START THE LEG DRIVE. THE QUAD'S CONTRACT TO FORCE THE KNEES TO FLATTEN, WHILE THE CALF'S CONTRACTION TRANSFERS THE DRIVE THROUGH THE BALLS OF THE FEET.

DIRECTION OF SEAT MOVEMENT

THE ILLUSTRATION ABOVE SHOWS THE MUSCLES INVOLVED (AND THE ROLE OF EACH) AT THE POINT OF THE CATCH AND THE START OF THE LEG DRIVE.

Anaerobic system

Anaerobic performance takes place when the athlete performs at extreme levels of energy output, to the extent that there is depletion of oxygen and a state of oxygen debt, which is created by the lactic energy pathway. There are two periods of time during a race when a rower is susceptible to the effects of entering the anaerobic state. The first period is soon after the start of the race and during the first 150 to 200m (163 to 218 yd), where maximum effort is being generated. Dependent on the boat class in which the race is being contested, this will last between 28 and 40 seconds.

The second period arises in the closing phase of the race where, naturally, maximum effort is being generated and sustained for approximately 50 seconds to one minute in the sprint for the finish. It is during this period that the rower re-enters the oxygen debt phase.

Anaerobic threshold

This is the point beyond which further increases in workload result in an accumulation of lactate and thus place severe constraints on any sustained output.

Lactate training

There are two prime methods for this training. The first is for the production of lactate and the second is for its removal. Thus there are two very different means of accomplishment for this training.

In the production-of-lactate phase the training plan will include achieving increased capacity for oxygen transport as well as increased utilization and a higher anaerobic threshold and better efficiency of VO_2 Max. In these sessions you may do six one-and-a-half-minute pieces with a short rest interval in-between each of, say, one minute to one-and-a-half minutes. The lactate accumulates throughout such a session.

A lactate building and removal session would comprise a high rate (or speed) as well as a high work (or load) output piece, followed by a low rate piece and, finally, light rowing for about 15 minutes.

The important skeletal muscles which are being stretched are illustrated below. These include the abdominal or stomach muscles, the muscles in the buttocks, the biceps and triceps, calf and quadriceps, shin muscles and the hamstring.

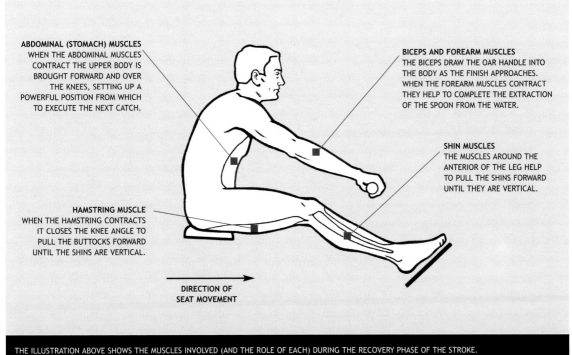

ABDOMINAL (STOMACH) MUSCLES
WHEN THE ABDOMINAL MUSCLES CONTRACT THE UPPER BODY IS BROUGHT FORWARD AND OVER THE KNEES, SETTING UP A POWERFUL POSITION FROM WHICH TO EXECUTE THE NEXT CATCH.

BICEPS AND FOREARM MUSCLES
THE BICEPS DRAW THE OAR HANDLE INTO THE BODY AS THE FINISH APPROACHES. WHEN THE FOREARM MUSCLES CONTRACT THEY HELP TO COMPLETE THE EXTRACTION OF THE SPOON FROM THE WATER.

SHIN MUSCLES
THE MUSCLES AROUND THE ANTERIOR OF THE LEG HELP TO PULL THE SHINS FORWARD UNTIL THEY ARE VERTICAL.

HAMSTRING MUSCLE
WHEN THE HAMSTRING CONTRACTS IT CLOSES THE KNEE ANGLE TO PULL THE BUTTOCKS FORWARD UNTIL THE SHINS ARE VERTICAL.

DIRECTION OF SEAT MOVEMENT

THE ILLUSTRATION ABOVE SHOWS THE MUSCLES INVOLVED (AND THE ROLE OF EACH) DURING THE RECOVERY PHASE OF THE STROKE.

Methods of high-level training

The workloads of top athletes deserve closer inspection. The greatest amount of their workload comes at a steady rate and over a long period of time. Sudden bursts of training will not provide any measurable long-term benefits. It takes consistent effort.

In setting the training plan the coach takes the athlete's progress over the years into account as well as the objectives for the coming season. The core for all rowing training programmes is steady rate and long distance, or low rate and medium work output rowing. Coaches are also now able to prescribe specific heart-rate goals for different exercises. Most coaches will encourage their athletes to use a pulse-rate monitor.

In establishing the training plan the coach will normally ensure that the programme is balanced and objective. As a result, 60–70% of the programme will focus on training the aerobic system, aiming to increase oxygen utilization in the recruited muscle fibres without the accumulated production of lactic acid.

The coach will also focus on improving the effectiveness of the rowing movement as well as the overall technical efficiency. Thus, 30–40% of the programme will be allotted to activities to work the anaerobic system, aiming to increase the capacity for oxygen transport, improve oxygen utilization, attain a higher aerobic threshold and a better efficiency of VO_2 Max.

Land-based training

There is a lot of useful literature written specifically on the subject of land-based training, which we don't have space for in this handbook. You need to exercise discretion in taking advice from gym instructors, as many are not acquainted with the specific requirements for rowing and very few instructors have the vaguest concept about the rowing stroke cycle. Rather take your advice from your club coach, who will have been carefully selected and appointed to the task because the position demands that the coach has acquired specialized knowledge and experience of the sport, as well as of the physiology related to the sport.

SEATED ARM PULLS ARE AN EXCELLENT EXERCISE FOR STRENGTHENING THE MUSCLES NEEDED IN THE DRIVE PHASE, ESPECIALLY THE ARMS AND SHOULDERS. CONCENTRATE ON KEEPING AN UPRIGHT POSITION SO THAT YOU DON'T STRAIN YOUR BACK MUSCLES OR DEVELOP BAD TECHNIQUE.

UPRIGHT ARM PULLS ALSO BUILD YOUR ARM STRENGTH FOR THE DRIVE PHASE, AS WELL AS BUILDING STAMINA TO PROVIDE CONTROL DURING THE EXTRACTION AND RECOVERY PHASES – THE LATTER DON'T REQUIRE POWER, BUT DO RELY ON ACCURACY FOR TIMING AND RHYTHM.

The ergometer

Time constraints, as well as the weather and wind, will often dictate whether or not a water outing can be undertaken. One thing is certain — rain, hail or snow, you will find that the ergometer can always be used to substitute a scheduled rowing outing on the water. Whether at home, the gym or in the boathouse, the ergo can become one of your most useful allies, particularly when unexpected situations affect your training plans. Apart from the weather issues, the ergo affords you enormous flexibility in being able to do your daily training at any time convenient to you.

Weight-training

Land training in the gymnasium will, inevitably, become an inclusive portion of your training load and, as a result, gymnasium sessions are included in a training plan. The workouts will be specific in their content, the mass to be lifted will be recommended by your coach, as will the number of sets and repetitions.

A typical land training programme should include:
- Strength training using weights
- Circuit training (with and without weights)
- Plyometrics (power training)
- Strength retention

The use of weights for training is essential, but you must ensure that you respect the equipment, for it can seriously injure you for life through one careless moment on your part. Beware of your ego getting the better of your physical capacity, or of succumbing to peer pressure. When it comes to weight training you should always err on the lighter side of the weight scale, instead gradually working towards the more substantial weights. Take one step at a time. Working with weights that are beyond your current level physically can result in a very serious injury, or you could seriously strain your muscles from over-exerting yourself. The latter would generally not be a long-term injury, but it could put you out of action long enough to provide a serious setback to your current season.

SEATED LEG PRESS REPETITIONS ARE AN EXCELLENT EXERCISE TO BUILD THE STRENGTH AND STAMINA OF THE BUTTOCK, CALF AND THIGH MUSCLES. THESE ARE USED TO PROVIDE THE EXPLOSIVE POWER NEEDED DURING THE CATCH AND DRIVE PHASE OF THE ROWING STROKE.

SEATED LEG EXTENSIONS ARE USEFUL FOR DEVELOPING STRENGTH AND STAMINA IN THE UPPER THIGH MUSCLES, WHICH PROVIDE POWER DURING THE LATTER PART OF THE LEG DRIVE. THE STOMACH MUSCLES ARE ALSO STRENGTHENED, HELPING TO CONTROL THE SLIDING SEAT.

No-one wants to be incapacitated by a muscular injury (which can make daily activities frustratingly awkward) when a sensible approach to weight training could see you improving at a steady rate.

When following a weight-training regime you should work with two or three crewmates. As a group you will be able to protect one another when using heavier weights. You will also find their assistance particularly helpful when doing weight routines such as squats and bench presses. With more people taking turns with the weights, it will permit a good amount of natural recovery time between each of your lifts or repetitions.

Flexibility and mobility
(Adapted from the FISA Coaching and Development programme)

Balance and poise are essential to good rowing and sculling technique, and all rowers have to be flexible and supple enough in order to be able to execute the rowing stroke well, in addition to being able to balance and control the boat in all types of weather conditions. The stretching of your muscles to add suppleness and increased movement and flexibility, as well as the range of the joint action in your body, is an essential part of the training process. All rowers are encouraged

BACK RAISES HELP TO STRENGTHEN THE MUSCLES IN THE BACK, SHOULDERS, STOMACH AND BUTTOCKS.

HAMSTRING STRETCHES ARE ESSENTIAL DUE TO THE CONSTANT BENDING OF THE LEGS IN SLIDE-SEAT ROWING.

COMBINED HAMSTRING AND GROIN STRETCHES ENSURE THAT THE CONSTANT STRAIGHTENING OF THE LEGS IN THE DRIVE PHASE DOESN'T LEAD TO STIFFNESS OR STRAINS.

HAMSTRING AND ABDUCTOR STRETCHES INCREASE FLEXIBILITY IN THESE MUSCLES AS WELL AS THE MUSCLES IN THE FOOT. DAILY REPETITION WILL SOON LEAD TO IMPRESSIVE LEVELS OF FLEXIBILITY.

to include stretching and flexibility movements in their training plans. Women are generally gifted with a degree of suppleness that males envy greatly, and men seem to have particular difficulty in the lower back and hamstring areas.

Make sure that you warm up properly before getting into the routine. Precede your workout exercises with at least 10 minutes of warm-up; this could include going for a short, light run or cycle, or taking an easy 'row' on an ergometer, before getting on with your workout programme. The flexing programme is aimed at warming and stretching the muscles.

PLEASE NOTE that you should *stretch*, don't strain! In addition, always carry out the warm-up exercises in an environment that is comfortable and dry, while at the same time being airy.

Development of mobility

There are three types of mobility training

- **Active exercises** are slow, sustained exercises for each joint action, and will assist you in maintaining your range of movement.
- **Passive exercises** include work where you use either your own body weight — or that of a training partner — or gym apparatus.
- **Kinetic exercises**, as well as combined strength and mobility exercises, relate to the dynamics of the sport and should only be used by mature athletes.

One also needs to work on specific movements that form part of the whole movement as exhibited through the stroke cycle. At the end of your training session it is essential that you warm down adequately.

Mobility exercises

In order to perform each exercise, first take up the positions indicated on this page by stretching the muscles until you start to feel the first sensation of pain. Hold your position for 20–30 seconds before progressively increasing the duration of your stretch. Work up to a 'hold time' of 45 seconds, then move on to 60 seconds, 75 seconds and, eventually, 90 seconds.

QUADRICEPS STRETCHES HELP TO LOOSEN THE MUSCLES NEEDED FOR THE POWERFUL DRIVE PHASE. THEY ALSO ENSURE AGAINST STRAINS THAT COULD ARISE FROM CONSTANTLY STRAIGHTENING THE LEGS.

SHOULDER STRETCHES LOOSEN THE SHOULDER, BACK AND — TO A LESSER DEGREE — THE BICEP MUSCLES. THESE A ROWER'S HARDEST-WORKING MUSCLES AND DEMAND SPECIAL CARE DURING STRETCHING.

HIP TWISTS HELP TO STRETCH YOUR BACK MUSCLES AND INCREASE MOBILITY OF THE SPINE. THIS IS PARTICULARLY USEFUL FOR ROWERS WHO TEND TO FAVOUR ONE SIDE MORE THAN THE OTHER. YOUR HEAD SHOULD FACE IN THE OPPOSITE DIRECTION TO YOUR PELVIS.

Rest and recovery from training

It is all very well to train hard, but it is equally important for you to include periods of rest and recovery into your training programme. It is imperative that you recognize the fact that physical adjustment and adaptation to sessions where progressive load has been applied takes place during recovery periods which should immediately follow the session or increased exercise. The higher your goals the greater the need for you to recognize that training and rest operate hand in glove with one another.

Post-competition rest is also important and, depending on the time of the competition within the annual cycle, a complete change to your routine may be the best remedy for recovery – for instance, when the expenditure of physical and emotional stress and pressure is high, after trials or a major domestic championship in which you want to excel, or for an international athlete – it may be Henley, Lucerne, the World Championships, or the Olympic Games. Whichever it is, the fatigue from the preparation, stress and competition will follow at the end of the competition and will be accompanied by an emotional 'down' phase, which is recognized in one of two forms. 'Post-euphoric depression' occurs when you have accomplished your goal; conversely, 'post-disappointment depression' is, naturally, when your goals have not been accomplished. Like food, rest provides the body with vital nourishment.

Specific training

All sport has its own specific requirements: speed for the sprinter, strength and power for the weightlifter, and endurance and power for the rower. Each discipline also has its own technique focus, as golfers, tennis players and gymnasts all have their own specific requirements from their technique. Consequently, your training will employ endurance and strength-based exercise to enhance your improvement as a rower.

'Cross-training' is the inclusion of a different sporting activity into your repertoire which can comfortably and effectively fit into your training programme. Activities such as cycling, running and swimming can enhance rowing fitness. Cross-training is also a great source for maintaining interest and motivation by adding diversity to your activities. However, in the final analysis there is nothing to replace the specific training that is required in the boat and on the water, and you shouldn't compromise on the amount of effort you put into 'boatwork'.

AN ERGOMETER IS AN ESSENTIAL PIECE OF EQUIPMENT FOR TRAINING ON BAD WEATHER DAYS. IT IS ALSO AN EXCELLENT TOOL FOR MEASURING FITNESS LEVELS, AS COMPUTERISED ERGOMETERS WILL ENABLE YOU TO MAINTAIN AN ACCURATE TRAINING LOG RECORDING THE DISTANCE 'TRAVELLED' IN EACH SESSION, SPEED, STROKE RATE AND TIME TAKEN.

Training diary

Keep a journal of your progress and of personal details, as it is both helpful and useful to reflect back on at later dates. Start by keeping a record of some of the most basic system indicators:

- Record your body mass daily and at the same time.
- Monitor and record your waking pulse rate every morning before you get out of bed.
- Other things to note: the regularity of your bowel movements and, for women, the regularity of your menstrual cycles.
- Do you drink enough water? About 200ml (7oz) every 15 minutes of the day, roughly 8 litres (2gal) per day, is the optimal intake you should consume.
- Do you get enough sleep and general rest?
- How did each boat outing or training session go?
- How did you feel and what improvements can be made after each boat outing or training session?
- What training you did

Progress and personal evaluation

It is all very well to train hard, but the question remains: 'Are you making good progress, and is the programme having the desired effect?' You need to know how to make these evaluations and how to measure your own progress. A pilot doesn't like flying blind, and along a similar vein there is no good reason for you to train aimlessly. Regular testing and evaluation is critical to your development – most people would agree that a race is the last place you want to be when you find out that things are not all quite right, technically, physically or in terms of your fitness, strength or endurance.

The consequences of using races for evaluation purposes may be that you psychologically destruct through loss of self-confidence via performances that belie your true potential. Evaluate your performances in training and practice so that you can perform to your full potential in those all-important races.

THE CHEESE-CUTTERS, STRAW HATS AND OLD SCHOOL TIE BRIGADE PRESENT A FORMIDABLE PRESENCE AMONG THE GALLERY AT THE ANNUAL HENLEY ROYAL REGATTA. SUCCESS AT HENLEY BRINGS PRAISE OF THE HIGHEST ORDER, WHILE THE FEAR OF ABJECT FAILURE AND THE EMBARRASSMENT OF A MAJOR RACE LOSS IS SUFFICIENT MOTIVATION FOR PARTICIPANTS TO PUT IN THAT EXTRA OUNCE OF EFFORT DURING TRAINING AS WELL AS ON RACE DAY.

Making contact

Rowing clubs usually have good training facilities and racing shells for the benefit of their members. They also usually have in their ranks experienced rowers with considerable insight into local conditions, who can offer sound advice, guide you in training and technique and help you progress on the water.

INTERNATIONAL AND NATIONAL ROWING ORGANIZATIONS

INTERNATIONAL

The International Rowing Federation (FISA)
- Av. de Cour 135, Case Postale 18, 1000 Lausanne 3, Switzerland
- Tel: (21) 617 8373
- Fax: (21) 617 8375
- E-mail: info@fisa.org
- Website: www.fisa.org

AFRICA
■ EGYPT
- **Egyptian Rowing Federation**
- 3 El Shawarabi St kasr El Nil, Cairo
- Tel: (2) 392 5498
- Fax: (2) 393 4350
- E-mail: egyrdfed@strnet.com.eg

■ SOUTH AFRICA
- **Rowing South Africa**
- PO Box 908, Parklands 2121, Gauteng
- Tel: (11) 643 8086
- Fax: (11) 484 1416
- E-mail: rowing.sa@mweb.co.za
- Website: www.pix.za/rowsa

■ ZIMBABWE
- **Rowing Association of Zimbabwe**
- PO Box CY 285, Causeway, Harare
- Tel: (4) 497 525
- Fax: (4) 668 250

ASIA
■ HONG KONG
- **Hong Kong China Rowing Association**
- Sha Tin Rowing Centre, 27 Yuen Wo Road, Sha Tin. N.T., Hong Kong
- Tel: (2) 699 7271
- Fax: (2) 601 4477
- E-mail: hkcra@hkstar.com
- Website: www.hkcra.org

■ JAPAN
- **Japan Rowing Association**
- c/o Kishi Memorial Hall, 1-1-1, Jinnan, Shibuya-ku, Tokyo 150 8050
- Tel: (33) 481 2326
- Fax: (33) 481 2327

AUSTRALASIA
■ AUSTRALIA
- **Rowing Australia**
- PO Box 4216, Penrith 2750
- Tel: (247) 294 500
- Fax: (247) 294 511
- E-mail: ausrowing@ausport.gov.au
- Website: www.rowingaustralia.com.au

■ NEW ZEALAND
- **Rowing New Zealand**
- PO Box 300-633, Albany, Auckland, New Zealand
- Tel: (9) 415 4618
- Fax: (9) 415 4617
- E-mail: nzrow@xtra.co.nz
- Website: www.rowingnz.org.nz

EUROPE
■ DENMARK
- **Danish Federation for Rowing**
- Skovalleen 38A, Postboks 74, 2880 Bagsvaerd
- Tel: (44) 440 633
- Fax: (44) 440 449
- E-mail: dffr@roning.dk
- Website: www.roning.dk

■ FRANCE
- **French Rowing Federation**
- 17 Boulevard de la Marne, 94736 Nogent sur marne Cedex
- Tel: (1) 4514 2640
- Fax: (1) 4875 7875
- E-mail: ffsa@avironfrance.asso.fr
- Website: www.avironfrance.asso.fr

■ GERMANY
- **German Rowing Association**
- Maschstrasse 20, 30169 Hannover
- Tel: (511) 980 940
- Fax: (511) 980 9425
- E-mail: ruderverband@t-online.de
- Website: www.ruderverband.org

GREAT BRITAIN
- Amateur Rowing Association
- The Priory, 6 Lower Mall, Hammersmith, London W6 9DJ
- Tel: (20) 8748 3632
- Fax: (20) 8741 4658
- E-mail: sophie@ara-rowing.org
- Website: www.ara-rowing.org

GREECE
- Hellenic Rowing Federation
- 22 Alex Koumoundourou Street, 185 33 Pireaus
- Tel: (1) 411 8011
- Fax: (1) 411 8088 / 413 4404
- E-mail: ekofns1@aias.gr
- Website: www.sportsib.com/ekofns

IRELAND
- Irish Amateur Rowing Union
- House of Sport, Longmile Road, Dublin 12
- Tel: (1) 450 9831
- Fax: (1) 450 2805
- E-mail: info@iaru.ie

ITALY
- Italian Rowing Federation
- Viale Tiziano 70, 00196 Roma
- Tel: (06) 323 3801
- Fax: (06) 368 58148
- E-mail: segreteria@canottaggio.org
- Website: www.canottaggio.org

SPAIN
- Spanish Rowing Federation
- Nuñez de Balboa 16, 1° Izq, 28001 Madrid
- Tel: (91) 4314 709/575 5920
- Fax: (91) 577 5357
- E-mail: e-mail@federemo.org
- Website: www.federemo.org

SWEDEN
- Swedish Rowing Federation
- Idrottens Hus, 12387 Farsta
- Tel: (8) 605 6435
- Fax: (8) 947 830
- Website: www.roddsverige.nu

SWITZERLAND
- Swiss Rowing Federation
- Brünigstrasse 182a, 6060 Sarnen
- Tel: (41) 660 7557
- Fax: (41) 660 9443
- E-mail: info@ruderverband.ch
- Website: www.ruderverband.ch

THE NETHERLANDS
- Netherlands Rowing Association
- Bosbaan 6, 1182 AG Amstelveen
- Tel: (20) 646 2740
- Fax: (20) 646 3881
- Website: www.nlroei.nl

NORTH AMERICA
CANADA
- Rowing Canada Aviron
- PO Box 17000, STN, Forces, Victoria, BC, V9A 7N2
- Tel: (250) 361 4222
- Fax: (250) 361 4211
- E-mail: rca@rowingcanada.org
- Website: www.rowingcanada.org

UNITED STATES
- US Rowing
- 201 S Capitol Ave, Suite 400, Indianapolis, IN 46225
- Tel: (317) 237 5656
- Fax: (317) 237 5646
- E-mail: members@usrowing.org
- Website: www.usrowing.org

SOUTH AMERICA
BRAZIL
- Brazilian Rowing Confederation
- Av. Borges de Medeiros, 1424 Gávea, Estádio de Remo da Lagoa, CEP 22770-000 Rio de Janeiro
- Tel: (21) 294 3342
- Fax: (21) 294 3342
- E-mail: cbr-remo@infolink.com.br

RUSSIA
- Russian Rowing Federation
- Loujnetskaia nab 8, Moscow 119871
- Tel: 7 095 201 0465
- Fax: 7 095 201 0128

Glossary

Backstay A metal brace, usually attached to the top of the pin to maintain the pitch.

Backstop The end of the slide nearest to the bows. The backstops is also the position a rower reaches at the finish of the stroke. At this point the legs will be stretched straight out and flat.

Blade Also referred to as the spoon, this is the end of the oar or scull that dips into the water.

Bow The front or forward end of the boat.

Bowside The starboard (right-hand) side of the boat.

Bow ball This is usually a white rubber ball attached to the sharp bow of the boat. The bow ball should not be less than 4cm (1.6in) in diameter.

Button A circular plastic collar which is pressed against the swivel and separates the oar's loom from its handle.

Catch Another word for the beginning of the stroke.

Coxless A two- or four-oared boat that doesn't have a coxswain to guide or motivate the rowers.

Coxswain A non-rowing member of the team whose function is to steer the boat, using a rudder, and to motivate and instruct the rest of the crew.

Crew The number of people who make up a rowing team – either two, four or eight.

Drive phase The part of the stroke cycle between the catch and the finish of the stroke. The blade is in the water throughout the drive phase.

Extraction When the spoons (or blades) are removed from the water at the end of the stroke.

Feather The spoon is turned flat and parallel to the water (feathered) during the recovery phase, except when square-spoon rowing. Feathering should only be done once the spoon has been extracted from the water.

Fin A metal, plastic or wood fin on the underside of the shell that prevents the boat from slipping sideways. It acts as a stabilizer, providing directional stability. Sometimes also referred to as a skeg.

Fixed seat Found in boats without sliding seats.

As a result, the legs stay straight, with the stroke being performed only by the upper body.

Frontstops The end of the slide that is nearest to the stern. It is also the position the rower reaches at the start of the stroke, with the knees fully bent and the seat at the front of the slide.

Gate The gate (a metal bar) is tightened by a screw to close the swivel over the oar.

Gunwale The upper edge of a boat's side.

Heel restraint The length of material connecting the bottom of the stretcher to the heel of the flexible shoe. This helps to stop the shoe from bending too far, allowing the rower to release the feet and exit the boat in an emergency.

Inboard The distance between the oar handle and the centre of the swivel pin.

Lateral pitch The pin's outward angle of inclination (measured from the vertical).

Length The length of a stroke (also reflects the imaginary arc of the spoon through the stroke).

Loom The part of the oar or scull that stretches from the spoon (blade) to the handle.

Outboard The part of the oar that 'rests' over the water, measured from the pin to the tip of the spoon.

Paddle A generic word for rowing or sculling.

Pair-oar A boat for two people – a pair-oar can refer to a boat with or without a coxswain.

Pin The pin closes the gate, helping to keep the oar in place. The pin is also the point at which the force of the drive phase propels the boat. Rigging calculations are taken from the pin's position.

Pitch This is the angle (measured from the vertical) that the spoon inclines during the drive phase. The pitch is determined by the lateral pitch, as well as the stern pitch.

Rake The angle of the stretcher (measured from the horizontal) – this is normally set at 45 degrees.

Rate of striking The number of strokes rowed in a minute (also called the rating).

Recovery phase Time span between the extraction

and the catch when the blade is out of the water.

Rhythm The optimum ratio between the recovery and propulsive phases; can vary from crew to crew.

Riggers The extensions that stretch from the saxboards out over the water, increasing the effective width of the boat and allowing more leverage of the oar. The riggers also support the swivel and pin.

Rigging The process of customizing a boat to fit the physical needs of a crew by adjusting the movable parts of the rigger and spoon, pin position, height of work and position of the footboards.

Saxboard The sides of the boat above the waterline which are strengthened where the riggers attach.

Scull A smaller oar that is used for sculling.

Shell Boats made of a smooth, moulded skin of wood or synthetic material.

Slide The runner apparatus on which a boat's sliding seat travels.

Span The distance between the pins on a scull.

Spoon The end of the oar or scull which dips into the water to drive the boat. Also called blade.

Spread The distance from the pin to the centre of the boat.

Squaring Turning the blade from a feather angle to approximately 90 degrees to the water. The blade should be square just prior to the catch.

Stern The rear end of a boat.

Stern pitch The sternwards angle of the pin (measured from the vertical).

Stretcher Adjustable footboard for pushing against, to which flexible shoes or clogs are attached.

Stroke A 'stroke cycle' consists of the catch, drive phase, finish and recovery. 'The stroke' is the rower or sculler who sits closest to the stern and who sets the crew's rhythm.

Strokeside The port (left-hand) side when facing the bow of the boat.

Swivel The U-shaped plastic mechanism attached to the rigger on which the oar or scull rests. The swivel rotates with the oar or scull in the stroke. The swivel rotates around the swivel pin.

Washing out When the spoon comes out of the water during the drive phase.

Watermanship A knowledge of boats and local water conditions in addition to the technical skills needed to propel a boat.

A SINGLE SCULLER POISED AT THE CATCH — IT CAN TAKE YEARS TO ACCOMPLISH THIS DEGREE OF BALANCE WITH ANY REGULARITY.

Index

Photographic Credits

Allsport/Touchline: pp 7, 8(top), 11, 14, 15, 18, 29, 54, 58 (top), 74 (bottom), 78; Bridgeman Art Library: p 8 (bottom); Colorsport: pp 13, 55, 91; Independent Rowing News: pp 35, 72, 79; Caroline Jones: pp 6–7; © IOC/Olympic Museum Collections: p 10; The River and Rowing Museum: p 9 ; Joel W Rogers: pp 2, 4–5, 12, 16 (bottom), 19 (bottom), 44 (bottom), 45, 46 (bottom), 56 (top), 59, 76 (bottom), 77, 82, 83.